A Deep Presence

A Deep Presence

13,000 Years
of Native American History

Robert G. Goodby

*Published in cooperation with
the Harris Center for Conservation Education
and the Historical Society of Cheshire County*

Peter E. Randall Publisher
Portsmouth, New Hampshire
2021

ISBN: 978-1-942155-40-9

Library of Congress Control Number: 2021909932

Printed in the United States of America

Published by:
Peter E. Randall Publisher
Portsmouth NH 03801
www.perpublisher.com

Book design by Grace Peirce

Cover art: *Tenant Swamp Paleoindian Site*,
by Miranda Nelken and Rex Baker III

Front cover photos (left to right):
Cheshire quartzite projectile point; stone tool recovered adjacent to the Swanzey Fish
Dam; fluted point from Ossipee Lake, New Hampshire (photos by Steve Bayly).
Mortar and pestle found along Lake Nubanusit, Hancock, New Hampshire (photo by
Ruth Wilder, courtesy of the Hancock Historical Society).
Elizabeth Sadoques, 1916 high school graduation photo (courtesy of Joyce Heywood
and the Historical Society of Cheshire County).

The Historical Society of Cheshire County is a nonprofit
educational institution dedicated to collecting, preserving and
communicating the history of southwest New Hampshire. To
learn more about the organization's diverse public programming,
visit www.hsccnh.org.

The Harris Center for Conservation Education is dedicated to promoting
understanding and respect for our natural environment through education of all
ages, direct protection and exemplary stewardship of the Monadnock region's natural
resources, conservation research, and programs that encourage active participation in
the great outdoors. Learn more at harriscenter.org.

To Tracy

Contents

Preface

I have been studying Native American history in the Monadnock region of south-western New Hampshire since 2000, when I was hired as an assistant professor of anthropology at Franklin Pierce College (now Franklin Pierce University). The idea for this book had its origin in talks I have given for the past fifteen years as part of the New Hampshire Humanities "Humanities to Go" program. This program supports scholars who present their work to a general audience, helping me move away from the technical language of my training to a more accessible and interesting way of talking about archaeology. In this book, I combine the roles of scientist and storyteller to present my version of the remarkable history of the Abenaki and their ancestors.

Throughout this book, I use the terms Indian, Native American, and Native interchangeably to refer in general terms to the original inhabitants of north-eastern North America. In doing so, I am following the lead of my friends and colleagues in the Native community, most colleges and universities, and practices followed by the National Museum of the American Indian, the National Congress of American Indians, and other organizations. When asked what they prefer to be called, most Native people will choose the name of their tribe or nation. This book focuses on the history of Native people in the Abenaki (pronounced A-BEN-a-ki or AB-e-nak-i) homeland. The word Abenaki derives from *Wabanaki*, or *Wôbanakiak*, which means "People of the Dawn Land," whose homeland extends over a broad area including modern-day Vermont, New Hampshire, and Maine. The traditional name for themselves in the Abenaki language, *Alnôbak*, is also used.

Acknowledgments

I am grateful for the support of Franklin Pierce University, including financial support from the Faculty Development Fund and the Monadnock Institute for Nature, Place and Culture, the latter of which drew from a grant from the Institute of Museum and Library Services. John Harris, Gerald Burns, Catherine Koning, and Rhine Singleton, all charter members of the Monadnock Institute, are thanked for their steadfast support and their appreciation of the importance of Native American history in the Monadnock region. Karen Brown, Carrie Desrosiers, Joleen Little, and Sharon MacCartney are thanked for their years of friendship and support and for helping with the logistics of my archaeology program. I am especially grateful to my Franklin Pierce archaeology students, who did most of the excavation described in these pages, and whose enthusiasm and energy made for so many enjoyable days spent travelling through time in the Monadnock region. Former students Cory Atkinson, Devin Batchelder, Yvonne Benney Basque, Alyssa Bergquist, Brian Deshler, Ellery Dowd, Ben Heaney, Matthew Labbe, Quinn Ogden, Kate Pontbriand, Celine Rainville, and Sarah Tremblay are thanked for their notable contributions to this research and for years of friendship and collegiality. Field assistants for Franklin Pierce field schools included my friends and colleagues Steve Bayly, Ed Bouras, Garrett Evans, Gail Golec, Mark Greenly, Dennis Howe, and Martha Pinello. Garrett, Mark, and Steve are also thanked for helping over the years with mapping, photography, and graphic production, and Paul Bock is thanked for his friendship, his contributions to fieldwork and research, and for keeping me supplied with top-quality field equipment.

The staff of the New Hampshire Division of Historical Resources (NHDHR), particularly Richard Boisvert, Edna Feighner, Tanya Krajcik, and Christine St. Louis, are thanked for their support. The NHDHR also provided financial support for the excavations at the Wantastiquet Mountain Site in 2005. Tonya Largy and Maine State Archaeologist Arthur Spiess conducted the faunal analysis for the projects described in this book, and Chris Dorion, Steve Pollock, and Heather Rockwell contributed their expertise to the research at the Tenant Swamp Site.

Preparation of the images included in this book was made possible by assistance from Steve Bayly, Mark Corliss, Garrett Evans, and Mark Greenly. A number of individuals and institutions helped in acquiring the images that appear here, including: Arthur Spiess (Maine Historic Preservation Commission), Jess Robinson (Vermont Division of Historic Preservation), Daniel Peters (Manchester Historic Association), Miranda Nelken (Keene Middle School), Andy Bullock (Mt. Kearsarge Indian Museum), Andy Cunningham (Franklin Pierce University), John and Donna Moody (Winter Center for Indigenous Traditions), Larissa Vigue Picard (Pejepscot History Center), Matthew Boulanger (Southern Methodist University), Karl Kreutz (University of Maine), Christopher Dorion (C. C. Dorion Geological Services, LLC), Ruth Wilder (Hancock Historical Society), Margaret Tamulonis (Fleming Museum of Art, University of Vermont), Sherry Gould (Nulhegan Band of Coosuk Abenaki), Lionel Chute (Connecticut River Joint Commissions), Victoria Bunker (Victoria Bunker, Inc.), Steve Hooper, Joyce Heywood, Lynn Murphy, and the *Keene Sentinel*.

Michelle Stahl, executive director of the Monadnock Center for History and Culture, is thanked for two decades of advice, support, and friendship. Lou Casagrande, Helen Frink, and John Harris provided valuable advice and guidance. Jesse Bruchac and Donna and John Moody are thanked for their assistance with questions about the Abenaki language and creation stories. Nancy Jo Chabot of the New Hampshire Antiquarian Society provided information on Native American remains once held by that institution. I am grateful for the assistance of two excellent in-house editors, Tracy Botting and Charlotte Schuttler, and the good folks at Peter E. Randall Publisher are thanked for their enthusiasm for this project and their superb editorial and production work.

I am fortunate to have received a fine education in anthropology and archaeology, and am particularly grateful to Doug Anderson, Richard Gould, and Patricia Rubertone of Brown University and Charles Bolian of the University of New Hampshire. Victoria Bunker was one of my earliest and most influential mentors and provided me with many opportunities in my archaeological career. I owe an enormous debt to the late Arthur Whipple for his friendship and insights into the Native American history of the Monadnock region.

The publication of this book was made possible by the generous financial support of the Harris Center for Conservation Education and the Historical Society of Cheshire County. Jeremy Wilson, Lisa Murray, Susie Spikol, and Brett Amy Thelen of the Harris Center and Alan Rumrill, Jenna Carroll, and Andrea Cheeney of the Historical Society of Cheshire County are thanked for their time and effort, and for appreciating the importance of Native history to an understanding of the Monadnock region.

Finally, I am grateful to my family for all their years of love and support.

CHAPTER 1
Introduction

Figure 1.1. Petroglyphs at Bellows Falls, Vermont. (Photograph by Gail Golec.)

It's there if you know where to look.

The drive up Route 12, north of Keene, New Hampshire, passes through beautiful farmland along the Connecticut River in Westmoreland and Walpole, the remnants of a Yankee agrarian culture fighting a long retreat against the spread of dollar stores and Tractor Supply Company outlets. This comes to an abrupt end in the village of North Walpole, a grimy industrial landscape dominated by half-abandoned railroad yards, where a small, rusted sign reading "To Indian Carvings" directs you to a trash-strewn dirt road along Bellows Falls (*Ktsi Pontekw*, or Great Falls, in the Abenaki language). After you walk through the weeds and look over the edge of a guardrail, abstract faces peer back at you, circular heads with round eyes, small mouths, and enigmatic horn-like protrusions. Like the people who made them, they are survivors, one of the few visible traces of a culture that extends back 13,000 years in New Hampshire and Vermont.

Their age is unknown, as stone carvings cannot be directly dated using radio-carbon dating. The carvings were seen by the first European settlers, who arrived in the late-eighteenth century with the end of the French and Indian wars, and the first written description of them is from 1789. In the nineteenth century, they were first covered with rocks during construction of the adjacent rail line, and then by waste from the nearby mills and snow from the streets of Bellows Falls. In the early 1930s, the local chapter of the Daughters of the American Revolution felt the carvings had become so obscured that they hired a stone carver to recarve them, and, in 1961, the local Chamber of Commerce had them outlined in yellow paint. These carvings stand as a metaphor for Native history in this area, almost invisible, badly damaged by the cruelties of history and conquest, but still there, ready to speak to anyone who listens.

There are many reasons for the near-invisibility of Native Americans in northern New England. Some of these have to do with the nature of the archaeological record they left behind, some are attributable to the erasure of Native history by the conquering culture, and some come from the survival strategies used by the Abenaki people to hide their identity from a hostile outside world and sometimes even from their own children.

Anyone interested in the history of Indian people in the Monadnock region of southwestern New Hampshire might start with Civil War hero Simon Griffin's *A History of Keene, New Hampshire*. Published in 1904 and long considered the standard work on the subject, Griffin wastes no time in pushing Indian people to the margins of local history, declaring in his first chapter that:

> The country was a wilderness, covered with dense forests through which no roads had yet been opened. Roving bands of Indians prowled those forests for game, or threaded them in single file, on habitual trails, to and from their more permanent abodes. For many years, but few Indians had lived in this immediate vicinity. (Griffin 1904:29)

This idea that Indian people didn't live in the region or have any enduring attachment to it had its obvious utility, eliminating awkward questions about how and why the land was forcibly taken from them in the eighteenth century, a seizure that was a prerequisite for the founding of every town in the region, including Keene. In reality, Indians were central to the origins of all these towns, as most were temporarily abandoned shortly after their founding due to the threat of Indian attack as Native people resisted colonial invasion. The name Monadnock itself, given to the lone mountain that dominates the landscape of southwestern

Figure 1.2. Abenaki ash splint fancy hamper, c. 1900. (Courtesy of the Mt. Kearsarge Indian Museum.)

New Hampshire, is an Abenaki word, meaning "the mountain separated" or "the mountain on its own." On Main Street in Keene, directly across from Keene State College, a metal plaque on a boulder marks the former location of a "Fort built in 1738 by the early settlers of Upper Ashuelot as a refuge from the Indians." Erected by the Daughters of the American Revolution (D.A.R.) only a few years after the publication of Griffin's book, the monument stamps the Abenaki as a hostile presence, but also undermines his assertion that the Indians weren't here and had no deep interest in the region.

The invisibility of Native American history is built into the cultural fabric of New England, but like Griffin's assertion and the D.A.R.'s plaque on Main Street, this claim has its own obvious contradictions. When I was teaching at the University of New Hampshire in the 1990s, I began the semester by asking my students (almost all of whom were from New England) to tell me when the first *human beings* arrived in New England. Semester after semester, the most common answer was 1620, harkening back to the Pilgrims (1492 was the second most common). Yet every student who answered 1620 could, if asked, tell me about the first Thanksgiving, an account that would prominently feature the generosity of the Native American hosts. This represents a profound erasure, and the even darker implication that Native history and human history are two different things.

Archaeology, which relies on material evidence and uses the scientific method, has the potential to undo the myths of written histories, and a central mission of archaeology in New England should be to overturn the invisibility of Native people. But the archaeological record is fragmentary, difficult to read, and easy for the lay person to overlook. The soils of New England are acidic, and organic materials such as wood, bone, and leather quickly decay. Today, Abenaki artists produce woodsplint baskets that command high prices at auction and are exhibited in museums across the region, but there is little chance that the basketry or textiles of their ancestors could be recovered in an archaeological excavation. The archaeological record is a jigsaw puzzle, waiting to be methodically reassembled from small fragments to see the larger whole, but preservation in northern New England is so poor that we may find only 10 percent of the original pieces, most of them are damaged, and we don't have a picture on the box to guide us. This makes the archaeology of Native people in New England unusually difficult, but also unusually rewarding every time some lost detail of the past can be brought back to life.

Along with poor preservation, the sites themselves are fragile. Except for frequently flooded terraces along major rivers, most of northern New England

Figure 1.3. Aerial photo from the late 1960s of industrial development adjacent to Amoskeag Falls in Manchester, New Hampshire, that destroyed some of the deepest, richest Native American archaeological sites in New England. (*Amoskeag Millyard, Canal Street, Manchester, Hillsborough County, NH*, from the *Historic American Buildings Survey* [Library of Congress].)

is covered by rocky, sandy glacial deposits that are upwards of 15,000 years old, settings where there has been little or no natural accumulation of soil. As a result, archaeological sites that are thousands of years old may be only a few inches below ground surface, making them easy to discover but leaving them vulnerable to destruction.

Nineteenth-century industry also contributed greatly to the destruction of Native American sites. Waterfalls were important locations for Native people, who gathered in the spring to harvest the huge numbers of migratory fish whose rapid passage upstream would be slowed when they hit the base of the falls. At Amoskeag Falls in Manchester, New Hampshire, early European settlers reported the fish were so abundant in the "eddy" at the base of the falls that fishing could be done with a basket. For thousands of years, this resource drew Native people, and Amoskeag in the mid-late spring would have hosted large numbers of people, related families from across the region who came to fish, renew family acquaintances, engage in important rituals, and create a stock of dried, smoked fish that could be used throughout the coming year. They left behind countless artifacts over eight or nine thousand years, which were covered by soil deposited in later floods that created some of the richest and deepest archaeological sites in all New England. But these same falls that drew the Native people also provided the power for the mills and factories of the Industrial Revolution, and as the industrial cities of New England flourished and grew, the archaeological sites along the river were destroyed long before there were archaeologists to look for them, making the notion of invisibility all the easier to sustain.

Discovering Archaeology

I've always been interested in the past, the idea that there is this world of hazy mystery, fading more and more from sight, that can be miraculously recalled with the right insight and effort. I have no idea why that appealed to me, but it did. I was fortunate to grow up in a family that was interested in history, took me to museums, and raised me in a house full of books with great pictures and stories, from a wonderfully illustrated children's edition of *Moby Dick* to books on World War II with horrifying pictures of the worst of human cruelty. As a very small child, I collected plastic dinosaurs, and after memorizing a set of illustrated flash cards, was even able to answer, to my parents' delight, a paleontology question on the old TV show *College Bowl*. Shortly after, I left my dinosaurs on the shelf and began to collect coins, wonderful bits of material culture whose precise dates, interesting designs, and styles that vary systematically from one country to the next make them an archaeologist's dream.

I grew up in central Connecticut on the east side of the Connecticut River, in a suburban town with a long history. It was only after I had moved away that I came to appreciate that it also had a remarkable archaeological record, with deeply-layered Native American sites on the river's flood plain. I had gotten hints of this, beginning with an elementary-school field trip to the local historical society, where, in the midst of the old farm equipment and dusty photographs, I was fascinated by a display case containing the skeleton of a very young Indian child, excavated from the terrace along the river and placed intact behind glass for visitors to see. I wondered about her life, and why she had died so early, and felt a sad emotional connection with this little person who, while from the same place, was from a time and a world so far away.

At age eight or nine, it did not occur to me that there was anything strange or disagreeable about her body having been taken from its resting place and put on public display for my edification.

A few years later, biking along the river with a friend, we came across an excavation of a Native site by members of the Archaeological Society of Connecticut. I was mesmerized and made a pest of myself for the rest of the day, running over with relics, real or imagined, that I'd found in nearby piles of dirt. But it was another decade until I seriously thought about archaeology again.

At age twenty-one, I was taking courses part-time at the University of New Hampshire in Durham, looking for a career and a direction, and found myself in an introductory-level course in cultural anthropology. There, I had the sort of experience I wish for all my students, but that so few ever have—the epiphany, the thunderbolt that makes everything clear. I was fascinated by what anthropologists had learned about humanity by studying the remote and exotic cultures of the world, showing how variable and contingent human behavior could be, and the huge array of paths human societies could take. All the taken-for-granteds of my world—monogamous marriage, war, the ever-present competition and hierarchy of capitalist society—were only the improbable outcome of one particular human journey that varied hugely from the paths of the thousands of other cultures. There were Himalayan societies where women had multiple husbands, all of them brothers; societies whose ethic of egalitarianism was so deeply embedded that their language lacked superlatives, words to denote "best," "strongest," "fastest"; militaristic societies in highland New Guinea whose battles would end by mutual agreement as soon as the first serious casualty was inflicted. I knew then that I was going to be a cultural anthropologist.

One of the first things any student of anthropology learns is that the discipline is made up of four fields whose combined insights, integrated with each other, create the basis for a holistic, universal science of the human species. Archaeology is one of those fields (cultural anthropology, biological anthropology, and linguistics being the other three). I dutifully took my introductory course in archaeology, found it less exciting than cultural anthropology, and was less than impressed watching the serious archaeology students spending hours at tables in our dingy archaeology lab (a former poultry research building) brushing and scrutinizing things that looked like non-descript pieces of rock recovered from local Native American sites. In my second year, I completed an independent study project, writing a lengthy paper (forty pages in the pre-computer era) on the cultural changes undergone by the local Abenaki Indians in the seventeenth century, a topic of my own choosing that allowed me to think like a cultural anthropologist without having to travel or live with people I didn't know. Since so much of the cultural change in that turbulent, bloody century involved material culture, with the explosion of the fur trade and the introduction of iron tools, guns, glass trade beads, brass pots, and European cloth, this topic was my entry into using *things* to do anthropology.

In the middle of the spring semester, I saw an advertisement for a summer lab assistant position at the state archaeology lab in Concord, and as this was my only chance at paid summer employment in anthropology, I applied and got the job. In a wonderful irony, I spent most of the summer sitting at a table in a dingy lab building, cleaning and scrutinizing things that looked like non-descript pieces of rock from local Native American sites, as well as huge bags of nails, brick fragments, and broken glass from an array of historic Euroamerican sites.

Every Friday, though, I got to go out in the field and help with the excavations of the State Conservation and Rescue Archaeology Program (SCRAP), and, at a Native American site in Tilton, New Hampshire, I had my second epiphany. Troweling through the sandy, rocky soils, I found a nicely made stone spear point, long and narrow, with a delicately shaped stem. Victoria Bunker, the director of the dig and one of my early mentors, identified it as a Stark point, dating to the Middle Archaic period, some 6,000–8,000 years ago. I was the first person in perhaps 7,000 years to have touched this object, which was exciting, but my second thought made me an archaeologist: how I could *use* this object to connect with that other person, to travel backwards through time and learn something about their life and bring that awareness back into the present. Because that's what archaeology is: not the pursuit of old things, but the use of those things to create an awareness of and a scientific, historical, and emotional connection to those who have gone before us. In this sense, archaeology is a wonderfully creative endeavor.

When I first fell in love with anthropology, I was working weekends doing landscaping and odd jobs for a retired philosophy professor who had a sprawling estate in Madison, New Hampshire, in the foothills of the New Hampshire North Country. When I showed up for work one Saturday morning, the old professor asked me how school was going, and, after listening to me enthuse about anthropology, he smiled and said, "You know, Robert, I've never been able to tell if anthropology is one of the sciences or one of the humanities." And he looked at me, expectantly. I don't remember what I stammered in response, but I know it was inadequate, and years later, when I had figured it out, I wished I could have that moment back, because the answer is important.

Science concerns itself with the study of the *natural* world. It presumes that this world behaves in an orderly, regular fashion, following universal principles and natural laws, and that nature has an objective reality, existing whether we are aware of it or not. Human beings, being animals, are part of the natural world, and there are many things about us that science can explain, including why we're taller than people were a century ago, how long ago our lineage split from the apes, and why human populations vary in skin color.

But human beings also live in a world of our own making, a cultural world where we create languages and origin stories, assign abstract meanings to things or experiences, and embrace beauty, emotion, and spirit in ways literature and art reveal much better than science. Since we inhabit both a natural and cultural world, with one informing the other, anthropology should not draw a line between the two, and an anthropological archaeology should try to address all aspects of the human past. In this book, I try to do just that, using science to discover some of the objective realities of Native history in the Monadnock region and as an inspiration and guide for writing imaginatively about what science can't show us.

CHAPTER 2
Who are the Native People?

One of the most frequent questions asked by non-Native people about the indigenous inhabitants of New Hampshire and Vermont, almost always in the past tense, is "what tribe were they"? People want a name, like Abenaki, Penacook, Pekwaket, or Sokoki, even if that name alone tells them little or nothing about the people in question. We are used to a world of nation-states, where (we are told) people have common national identities, speak common languages, share a common culture, and have clear geographic boundaries: nice clean lines on a map, that separate them from their neighbors and show you where one people begins and another ends. Of course, even for people of European descent, this idea of national identity is a recent and still contested convention, but it makes things simple if you have a nice, neat name you can walk away with and be spared an extended academic discussion on the nuances and complexities of identity. So, we provide names. The most common name for the Native people discussed most in this book is Western Abenaki, a people whose traditional homeland, known as Ndakinna, encompasses New Hampshire, Vermont, and parts of northern Massachusetts and southern Quebec.

With this question of identity, we have to start by discussing who Native Americans are. Even that is a far more complicated question than it used to be when I discovered anthropology. The old story was that most Native Americans were the descendants of early immigrants from Asia, biologically modern *Homo sapiens* coming over a land bridge connecting Siberia and Alaska in the last part of the Pleistocene epoch, some 13,000 or 14,000 years ago. These people spread rapidly throughout two empty continents, and their descendants make up most of the modern Native cultures. A second, later wave of migration was also posited, bringing speakers of the Athapaskan languages, found today mostly in northern Canada but also in the Navajo and Apache people of the American southwest, and a third, still later wave, brought the Inuit people of the far north.

The old story began to collapse under the weight of new archaeological evidence in the 1980s that showed humans were in the Americas thousands of years earlier than previously believed. Genetic evidence now shows a picture of considerable complexity, with rapid waves of expansion and immigration by many distinct populations who came into contact with each other, swapping genes and culture and giving rise over thousands of years to the amazing array of distinct Native American cultures in the Americas at the time of European contact.

The Native people of New England spoke closely related languages and dialects of the Algonquian language family, a diverse group of languages spoken by hundreds of distinct societies spread over thousands of square miles of eastern and central North America. Early European explorers and colonists noted that the various Indian dialects of New England were mutually intelligible, but less so as the geographic distance between speakers increased. As with social and political boundaries, clear linguistic boundaries did not exist in New England, and the interconnections and similarities far outweighed any differences. Historian Lisa Brooks writes in detail of these connections in her book *Our Beloved Kin*, showing how close ties of kinship permitted Narragansett and Wampanoag people from southeastern New England to find refuge among their Abenaki relatives in southwestern New Hampshire during King Philip's War (1675–1676). These complexities give lie to the bold lines that separate the "tribal" territories of New England in the 1978 *Smithsonian Handbook of North American Indians* and are better depicted on more recent maps created by Abenaki scholars that show place names without insisting on lines between communities or people.

But most folks still want a name to put on the Native people of a particular area, and the historical and anthropological literature is filled with them. These names are often confusing and unreliable, many of them being place names that the Europeans applied to whatever people they happened to encounter there. In the Monadnock region, these names include Contoocook in the east and Sokoki, Squakheag, or Sokwakik in the west. These were taken by historians as the names of distinct political entities ("tribes"), each assumed to have its own leader and defined political boundaries. Adding to this confusion is the fact that the communities Europeans were interacting with were not the traditional ones of the pre-Contact period, but the survivors of a horrendous pandemic of European origin in 1616–1617 that killed 90 percent or more of all the Native people from Cape Cod through Maine. These survivors came together in new communities in a world profoundly changed from the one they knew only a few years before. Their survival then, and over the next four centuries, was made possible by support from kin and the ties that linked different communities, not by the tribal identities that separated them. When we insist on placing the Native people of New England in small tribal boxes, emphasizing boundaries and differences rather

Figure 2.1. Map of a portion of the Connecticut River valley with Abenaki place names for the some of the locations mentioned in this book. (Courtesy of the Connecticut Joint Rivers Commission; Lisa Brooks, Donna Roberts Moody, and John Moody, "Native Spaces," in *Where the Great River Rises*, ed. Rebecca A. Brown, pp. 133–137. Hanover, NH: Dartmouth University Press, 2009.)

than similarities and connections, the real complexities and strengths of Native societies in New England are lost.

It becomes even more distorted when we try to place people from thousands of years ago in those same ill-fitting tribal boxes, as if nothing in their lives changed over those vast expanses of time. In a general way, the people living in New Hampshire and Vermont thousands of years ago were almost certainly the ancestors of the historic and modern Abenaki people, as there is little evidence for the region being abandoned or subject to invasion from outside before the seventeenth century. But how they thought of themselves is a difficult question to answer when the data comes from chipped stone, broken ceramics, and the remains of cooking fires. For archaeologists, knowing who these people were will never be completely possible, and if we're to say anything at all it will be through a mix of science, history, imagination, and, maybe, from talking to their descendants.

Archaeologists tell one story about Native history. The Abenaki have their own history and creation story, one that does not rely on archaeological data but on accounts that have been passed on orally for countless generations. Parts of these Abenaki stories can co-exist comfortably with the stories told by archaeologists, while others cannot. Like the traditional knowledge of any people, these accounts are not static, but can be altered and transformed in the telling over the years, and slightly different versions might be found from one community to the next. Common elements connect all these stories, including the idea that the Abenaki people were created here, in Ndakinna, by the creator Ktsi Niwaskw, in a land whose contours were shaped by the transformer Odzihozo at the beginning of time. Some traditional stories describe floods that may be cultural memories of glaciers melting, and scholars have long recognized that some of the characters in these stories, like giant beavers or hairy elephant-like creatures, may be ancient memories of giant Pleistocene mammals, like the mammoths and mastodons that flourished in Ndakinna more than 10,000 years ago. The extent to which these traditional stories and the archaeological narratives can co-exist or even inform one another has only recently been explored.

CHAPTER 3
Opening the Puzzle

To be an archaeological site, a place must be one where people did something in the past and, crucially, where their activities left traces that can be seen and interpreted years later. It's this last part that's difficult, as much of what humans do leaves few traces, and many of the important events in our lives—the birth of a child, a first kiss, sitting with an elder as they depart this world—leave no traces at all. The archaeological record, the sum of all the material traces of our lives that do survive, is often coarse-grained, and the garbage from our everyday activities tells us far more about diet and technology than about meaning, emotion, or our spiritual world.

It's a beginner's mistake to think that every archaeological site is like Pompeii or the wreck of the *Titanic* where a single moment is encased, preserved in time, waiting for an archaeologist to come along. Occasionally, we find small sites that really do reflect a single point in time—an afternoon of fishing or an overnight camp site—where we can think of everything as happening all at once. More often, Native sites are a composite of many points in time spanning days, weeks, or even months, repeated over centuries and millennia. For much of their history, the Native people of New England were what anthropologists call hunter-gatherer bands, small groups of related people who took their sustenance from nature in its wild form, and, with the exception of the dog, did not rely on domesticated plants or animals for their subsistence. But they were not, as Simon Griffin implied, wandering nomads. Instead, they moved from place to place regularly throughout the year, year after year, camping at waterfalls for spring fishing and moving to smaller camps in the fall to hunt deer and collect nuts. They were mindful of the places they chose to live, looking for settings with ready access to clean water, near traditional trails or canoe routes, and with terrain that was level and underlain by dry, sandy soil that would not turn to mud when it rained.

These movements were based on a deep, traditional knowledge of the environment, combining detailed knowledge of botany, zoology, and geology that sustained Native people in New England from their arrival 13,000 years ago until the present. Because it worked, because it made sense, Native people came back to the same places generation after generation, places that would be bound up with the memories of earlier stays and that would, in time, be given particular names. These places were not just about food. Trips to quarry sources to find the scarce, fine-grained stones they made tools of were also part of this calculus of seasonal movements. And all of this took place against a backdrop of human relationships. One of the basic rules of bands is exogamy—the idea that you should marry someone from another band, from outside your group. This rule transformed what might have been isolated communities into extensive networks of relatives, a kin-based geography that identified not just physical places but locations where your relatives would be at particular times of year. People planned their movements not just to find food but to meet family, and these patterns of land use and social interaction had deep roots, lasting for centuries or millennia.

What this left behind was an archaeological landscape made of the overlapping, co-mingled remains of hundreds of different moments in time where small groups of people repeatedly returned to the same places. There may be lots of artifacts on a given site, but they can be difficult or impossible to sort into their separate moments. This is compounded by the fact that most New England sites are in shallow soils. Unless you're on a river terrace where regular floods deposit layers of fine silty sand, what you're likely to encounter is a few grudging inches of topsoil before hitting sandy, rocky deposits laid down during the retreat and melting of glaciers some 14,000 to 16,000 years ago. As a result, tens of thousands of artifacts from hundreds of occupations over 8,000 or 9,000 years can be compressed into a foot of soil, which in turn is churned by animal burrows, the occasional toppling of trees, rocks moved by frost, and the annual plowing of farm fields that accompanied the European invasion of the seventeenth century. The jigsaw puzzle box, with its missing pieces and unhelpful box top, is muddied even further because the box, in fact, contains pieces from many different puzzles all mixed together.

The exceptions to this have been crucial to understanding Native history. Often, our oldest sites, dating to the end of the last glacial advance, were not reoccupied by later people who inhabited a radically different environment and made different decisions about where to camp and settle. And on river flood plains, superimposed layers of artifacts from different time periods show intriguing shifts in artifact forms, access to quarry sources, and changing patterns of interaction with Native cultures across eastern North America. I spent my second summer as an archaeologist working on the Eddy Site in Manchester, where a remnant of a deep, rich river flood plain site repeatedly occupied for 8,000 years had

Figure 3.1. The excavation of the Eddy Site in Manchester, New Hampshire, in 1985, revealed six feet of deposits spanning 8,000 years of Native American history. Left to right: Mike Burt, Victoria Bunker, and Robert Goodby. (Courtesy of Victoria Bunker.)

miraculously survived, wedged between two gas stations on the edge of a four-lane highway.

As a rule, though, sites that are rich in artifacts are often less revealing than smaller, ephemeral sites where you can clearly see single points in time. The Whitcomb Bridge Site in Dalton, New Hampshire, was an example of this, being both one of the most elegant sites I ever worked on and one of the humblest. Situated on a narrow shelf of moderately well-drained soil along the Connecticut River, the site produced only a handful of artifacts, with the highlight being the remains of a small cooking hearth surrounded by a few hundred flakes of stone from a

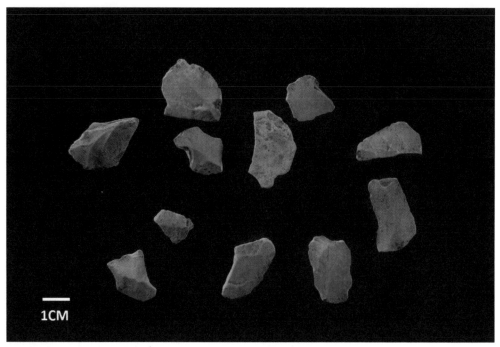

Figure 3.2. Shale flakes from the Whitcomb Bridge Site, Dalton, New Hampshire. (Photograph by Steve Bayly.)

single episode of tool making. Charcoal from the hearth was radiocarbon dated, placing its age between 3,265 and 3,625 years before present, at the end of the Archaic period. The small size, the low number and variety of artifacts, and their clustering around a single small hearth made it look like an overnight stay, where a small group of people had stopped on their way down the river, pulled the canoe ashore, and spent the night, cooking a meal or two and leaving the next day. In this respect, it was no different from thousands of other small sites, except that it was not overlain by artifacts from subsequent visits, so we could really focus on that single moment. And then there was the stone.

The few hundred flakes, created when a piece of stone was shaped into a tool by striking off chips, were of a weathered grey material that looked superficially like weathered hornfels from eastern New Hampshire, but they were so soft, with a consistency like wet talc, that gently brushing them left striations in the stone. Geologists Barbara Cologero and Wallace Bothner identified the stone as shale, which was not native to this area, and its powdery surfaces were not weathered, but naturally this soft. It flaked just like chert, rhyolite, hornfels, or other stones commonly used by Native people, only more easily and with less effort, but, being so soft, it would have made nearly useless tools. The only real purpose it might have had was for practice by young children, who could hone their skills with an easy-to-work material and not have to waste the more useful stone needed by their elders. At Dalton, then, we could glimpse a single moment in time when a child sat down at this campsite and took another small step on the years-long journey to becoming a skilled toolmaker. Had this been a richer site, with thousands of artifacts from dozens of different episodes of occupation mixed together, that moment in time would have been lost, and we wouldn't know that there was such a thing as children's stone.

While sites are the places archaeologists can see, the geography of Native people extended far beyond those locations. Significant or sacred places, such as mountaintops, might never be visited, so, while important, would have no archaeological sites on them. Other places had significance bound up in history and memory. Places where the dead were laid to rest would be remembered and possibly avoided. One such place was in Holderness, New Hampshire, along the Squam River, a short stretch of water connecting Big Squam and Little Squam lakes; one of those places whose level terrain, dry, sandy soil, access to major waterways, and beautiful views of the surrounding mountains made it an ideal setting for Native people to live. Archaeological work done before the construction of a public boat launch uncovered clusters of hearths and artifacts that showed over 1,000 years of repeated occupation. Most of these hearths were typical of Native habitation sites, containing the charred bones of deer, turtle, and canid (dog or wolf), as well as burned fragments of acorns and other nuts and broken or worn-out stone tools. But the last occupation, dating to around 2,900 years ago, was different. Here, the hearths were unusually large, constructed from small boulders, and contained very few artifacts or bones. These hearths may have been built as part of funerary rituals, as the remains of a young woman and the fragmentary remains of an unknown number of other individuals were also recovered from the site. And for the next 2,600 years, despite its ideal setting and the presence of Native people throughout the Lakes Region, the site remained unoccupied.

Keeping Track of Time

When archaeology first began in the mid-nineteenth century, it had little basis for estimating the age of artifacts, and often assigned little time depth to the Native cultures here, continuing a long-held and self-serving belief that the Indian peoples had only recently arrived, and therefore had no greater claim to the land than the Europeans. This changed in the early twentieth century, when the Paleoindian Clovis and Folsom cultures were recognized in the American southwest and their beautifully crafted fluted points were found embedded in the bones of extinct ice-age animals. Shortly after, similar points were recognized across eastern North America, including in collections from New England.

Figure 3.3. Fluted point from Ossipee Lake, New Hampshire. Dating to the Paleoindian period, this point was made between 10,000 and 11,000 years before present. Shown at actual size. (Photograph by Steve Bayly.)

The idea that New England was a marginal, nearly empty landscape persisted, with the notion of a long abandonment following the Paleoindian period that was not completely disproved until the 1980s. Crucial to this was the use of radiocarbon dating, which, by measuring the decay of radioactive isotopes, could be used to date burned wood, bone, or other organic materials recovered from Native sites. Radiocarbon dating is not pinpoint precise but produces dates in radiocarbon years before present (or BP), expressed as a range that might be as much as 150 or 250 years. These dates are then calibrated to adjust for fluctuations in atmospheric carbon-14 over time and presented as a range of calendar years before present, with AD 1950 used as present so dates don't have to be continually adjusted with the passage of time. With this technique, burned wood fragments from a hearth could be radiocarbon dated, and that date could be extended to any stone or ceramic artifacts found in or next to it.

Using this technique, in the 1970s, the Neville Site in Manchester, New Hampshire, was shown to have a series of well-defined occupations, each with its own distinct style of artifacts, that dated back almost 8,000 years before present. In the next decade, more of this work would narrow and eventually close the gap between the Paleoindian period and more recent occupations, showing the region has been inhabited continuously by Native Americans for more than 12,000 years.

Artifact styles are key to determining the age of sites. Just as automobile styles have changed over time, as a result of evolving taste, influences from abroad, individual innovation, and changing function, so did some of the tools made by Native people. The best known of these artifacts is what the lay person recognizes as an "Indian arrowhead," some of which were more likely spear points while others were multi-purpose tools mounted on a short wooden or antler handle. Archaeologists have worked out the age of these artifact styles by radiocarbon dating the layers of soil they are found in, or the hearth, storage pit, or grave from which they were recovered.

However, lacking the cultural and historical context we have for understanding changes in automobile style, what we haven't figured out is *why* these styles change, and, even more remarkably, why they do so over such broad areas. The fluted points of the Paleoindians were used across North America, and the stylistic changes in point forms documented at the Neville Site happened at essentially the same time and in the same fashion all down the Atlantic seaboard from Maine to Georgia. The distinctive points of the later Woodland period are used in common by cultures from New England through the mid-Atlantic and out to the Great Lakes, crossing different environments and important cultural and linguistic boundaries, notably between the Iroquoian and Algonquian speaking peoples, who had markedly different cultures and developed a bloody rivalry in the historic period.

Archaeologists, like our historian cousins, recognize changes over time that seem to mark important shifts in human technology, politics, or thought. As historians apply terms like the Enlightenment, the Medieval period, the Victorian Age, or the eighteenth century to make talking about history easier, archaeologists have come up with their own framework to manage and organize the past. In New England, it's a relatively simple scheme, starting with the Paleoindian period, followed by the long Archaic period (subdivided into Early, Middle, Late), the Woodland period, and the Contact period, marked by the earliest contacts with Europeans beginning in the late 1400s and early 1500s.

Table 3.1. Timeline of Native American Archaeological Periods in New England

Period	Years Before Present (BP)	BC/AD
Contact	300–500	AD 1,500–1,700
Late Woodland	500–1,200	AD 800–1,500
Middle Woodland	1,200–2,000	AD 1–800
Early Woodland	2,000–3,200	1,200 BC–AD 1
Late Archaic	3,200–6,000	1,200–4,000 BC
Middle Archaic	6,000–8,000	4,000–6,000 BC
Early Archaic	8,000–10,000	6,000–8,000 BC
Paleoindian	10,000–13,000	8,000–11,000 BC

Any framework that looks this orderly should arouse suspicion. These periods conveniently correspond to millennia or, at best, centuries, which is odd, given that they are applied to the history of people who recognized no such distinctions. The framework is, of course, an abstraction, a device employed to make analysis and discussion easier. It is important to know what these divisions are based on to understand the archaeology of any region, and in New England, they are often not based on much. The divide between the Archaic and Woodland periods, which in the Midwest is related to the appearance of mound-building traditions, agriculture, population increase, and intensive, long-distance social interaction, is in New England only heralded by the addition of conical-shaped, undecorated ceramic vessels to the technological repertoire. Likewise, the divisions within the Archaic and Woodland periods are based almost entirely on the appearance or disappearance of certain styles of stone tools or particular forms and decorative styles of ceramics, and we have little or no idea what (if anything) these have to do with any larger changes in the lives of the people who made them. We use artifacts as a basis for our time periods because they are what we have: they do not decay, we find a lot of them, and we can determine their age with radiocarbon dating. *Why* these styles change (or don't), for the most part remains a mystery.

Water

One of the questions I'm often asked is how I know where to look for sites, and for the most part, it's a fairly simple question. Sites tend to be close to water, where the terrain is level and sandy soils help keep the ground dry. All people need good sources of water for washing, drinking, and cooking, and this is provided by the lakes, rivers, and streams that are found across the landscape of northern New England. Water is also a source of food, not only fish but the birds and animals that are drawn to it as well. Water also enables travel for people with boats, and the Native people of New England used streams and rivers as their highways and roads, travelling annually over these routes on their seasonal round, or taking long trips to visit distant kin in other parts of the northeast. Two types of boats were used. Dugout canoes, made of large white pines, navigated the larger lakes and rivers, while birchbark canoes, whose light weight let them ride high in the water, were ideal for faster moving streams and shallow, rocky rivers. These craft were so well-suited for the waterways of New England that they were both immediately adopted by the European colonists in the Contact period.

The suitability of the larger dugouts for long-distance travel is suggested by an account from the 1640s by the founder of Rhode Island, Roger Williams. Living with the Narragansett and speaking some of their language, he described Narragansett leaders, or sachems, taking dugout canoes all the way down Narragansett Bay into the open ocean, west through Long Island Sound, and north up the Hudson River to modern-day Albany. Here they would meet with the Mohawk before returning home: a round-trip journey of some five hundred miles. With these boats, Native people could be part of an interconnected world that stretched for hundreds and even thousands of miles, an insight that does much to explain the similarities in artifact styles seen for thousands of years across much of eastern North America.

Figure 3.4. Dugout canoe recovered from Laurel Lake, Fitzwilliam, New Hampshire, and housed at Franklin Pierce University. Dugouts like these were used by the Abenaki and copied by early European settlers. (Photograph by Andy Cunningham, Franklin Pierce University.)

At the same time they could travel great distances, the Native people of northern New England, like most people, spent most of their lives in the same general area, a homeland that they knew intimately from hundreds of generations of accumulated experience and lifetimes of seasonal travel. Archaeologist Dean Snow, in his 1980 book *The Archaeology of New England*, argued that river drainages (the river, its tributaries, and all the land that drained into them) could be thought of as cultural containers, as, given the difficulty of travelling overland, people tended to interact far more with people within their own river drainage than with people from adjacent drainages. As a result, cultural differences between people in adjacent drainages would emerge over time, reflected, perhaps, by differences in dialect, or in the style of house construction or ceramic decoration. The river drainage model is an interesting, logical, and potentially powerful idea, but long before archaeologists had good data to support it, we assumed it was valid, and we've never looked back.

Figure 3.5. Eighteenth-century Abenaki birchbark canoe, Maine. (Courtesy of the Pejepscot History Center.)

Stone

Archaeologists in New England can be forgiven if we seem to be obsessed with all things made of stone. After all, most of the artifacts we find are stone, since stone preserves so well. (A tee shirt I saw for sale at a national archaeology meeting proclaimed, "Love is fleeting . . . but stone tools are forever.") Stone, if read properly, can give us insights into many aspects of Native life, from childhood and travel to work patterns and social networks.

Stone tools fall into two broad categories. The first, ground-stone tools, are typically made from dense igneous rocks like diorite or andesite, picked up as cobbles in stream beds and shaped through a laborious process of grinding and pecking with another piece of hard stone. Ground-stone tools are typically for heavy work: axes for felling trees, gouges and adzes for hollowing out dugout canoes, mortars and pestles for grinding seeds and nuts, and large sinkers for weighing down fishing nets. Each of these tools takes dozens of hours to make, and a large, finely made ground-stone axe may reflect ninety or one hundred hours of tedious labor.

Figure 3.6. Broken stone gouge from the Swanzey Fish Dam Site, Swanzey, New Hampshire. (Photograph by Mark Corliss.)

1 cm

Figure 3.7. Stone axe from the Wantastiquet Mountain Site, Hinsdale, New Hampshire. (Photograph by Garrett Evans.)

While these tools were important, they are only infrequently found by archaeologists, as there were relatively few of them in the tool kit of any family, much the way a typical New Englander today might own thirty screwdrivers but only one pickaxe. Far more common are flaked-stone tools, made of fine-grained stones like rhyolite or chert. With these materials, in a process called flintknapping, chips are quickly detached by striking with a hammerstone or an antler baton, or with pressure by prying off fine chips with the sharpened tip of an antler tine, not unlike how a sculptor might use a chisel to shape wood or marble. This continues until the desired form is achieved, and the maker then departs, leaving hundreds or even thousands of small, sharp-edged flakes of stone as evidence of their work. Flaked-stone tools are smaller, and include almost all the arrowheads, spear points, knives, and scrapers that dominate most museum collections. Looking at the surface of these tools, you can see the scars where the last flakes were removed, shallow channels separated by arrises, or ridges. Flakes can only be removed by striking the edge of the piece being worked and only if that edge has an acute angle. When a flaked-stone tool has been made bifacially, that is, with flakes taken off both sides, it leaves a sinuous edge, marking the converging starting points of dozens of individual flakes.

Figure 3.8. Mortar and pestle found along Lake Nubanusit, Hancock, New Hampshire. The pestle is approximately nine inches long. Mortars like this are often found in areas that had stands of nut-producing trees; acorns in particular had to be shelled, pounded into meal, and soaked in water before they would be edible. In the last 800 years before European contact, they may also have been used to grind corn. (Photograph by Ruth Wilder. Courtesy of the Hancock Historical Society.)

It's also important to remember that for most of these stone tools, we're only seeing part of them. Most would have been attached to wooden handles of various sizes, or arrow or spear shafts if they were used for hunting. These handles and shafts don't survive our acidic soils, leaving, again, an empty space in the jigsaw puzzle for our reason and imagination to fill in. It is equally important to remember that many of these tools had complicated lives—in an environment where high-quality stone was scarce, they would have been continually resharpened, repaired, and even converted to another purpose. A large knife might break

Figure 3.9. Stone tools from the Wantastiquet Mountain Site showing flake scars, arrises, and sinuous edges. Because of their distinct styles, their age can be estimated. The tool on the left dates between 1,400 and 1,800 years before present; the center, 2,000–5,000 years before present; and the right, 3,000–4,000 years before present. (Photograph by Garrett Evans.)

in half during heavy use, and, rather than discarding the broken halves, one would be converted into a scraper and the other into a spear point, each of which had its own cycle of use and reuse before eventually being repurposed again, lost, or discarded. Only through careful examination and understanding the process of flintknapping is it possible to see hints of this, and to see that even individual tools can have their own interesting history.

The flakes from stone toolmaking are found at almost every Native site in New England, because knowing how to make, repair, and resharpen these tools was a basic life skill. These flakes can range from a handful of small chips left by quickly resharpening a dull scraper to a few thousand flakes left behind by an afternoon's toolmaking. My personal record was finding over eleven thousand flakes in a 50-cm-square shovel-test pit excavated next to a small quarry site in southern Massachusetts. But what can you learn from these chips of stone? It turns out, quite a bit. The size of the flakes reflects the stage of toolmaking. Making a tool from a cobble coming directly from a quarry or picked up in a streambed will leave flakes of a range of sizes, larger ones from the initial shaping down to tiny retouch flakes left by the last stages of edge sharpening. If existing tools are only being resharpened, in contrast, all the flakes will be small and there will be relatively few of them. In general, the more abundant a material is and the closer people are to its source, the larger the flakes will be, whereas exotic materials from far-distant quarries often arrive as finished or near-finished tools, leaving no evidence of manufacture and only the occasional small flakes from sharpening and repair.

The type of stone found is a rich source of information on many aspects of Native life. To make decent flaked stone tools, you need stone that is cryptocrystalline, so fine-grained that its crystal structure can barely be discerned, so that when it is struck the resulting force waves will travel through the stone in a uniform, predictable fashion, unimpeded by large inclusions of other minerals or irregularities. There is relatively little of this stone in New Hampshire, and much of what there is comes from specific local sources, each with a distinct visual appearance and chemical makeup. One of the best known is the Mount Jasper quarry outside of Berlin, New Hampshire, where a wide seam of rhyolite extends through the top of a small mountain. So many tons of this material were taken out by Native people, beginning in the Paleoindian period and continuing for the next 10,000 years, that they created a large cave that today is listed on the National Register of Historic Places. The stone itself is light tan with small circular inclusions called spherules and is recognizable even when it occurs on sites hundreds of miles from the source

There are a handful of other sources of usable stone. In and around Jefferson, New Hampshire, fifteen miles to the west of Mount Jasper, a similar rhyolite was found in the glacial till. To the south and east, in the town of Ossipee, a buff-colored rhyolite originating in the eroded remnants of an ancient volcano was used by Native people and is found on sites throughout the New Hampshire Lakes Region and all the way down the Merrimack River valley, but rarely outside this area. Another distinct material is hornfels, a metamorphized siltstone found in streambeds in Ossipee and Tamworth, where the Merrimack and Saco river drainages come together near the Maine-New Hampshire border. Hornfels is jet black in its original form, but once flaked and exposed to air, it weathers to a grey-green color. Like the Ossipee rhyolite, this material is found through the Lakes Region and the Saco and Merrimack river valleys, but far less frequently in sites along the Connecticut River. While these local materials tend to predominate on New Hampshire sites, there is a small but consistent number of tools from more remote quarries: Kineo rhyolite and Munsungun chert from northern

Figure 3.10. Looking out from inside the Mount Jasper Quarry, Berlin, New Hampshire. (Photograph by Garrett Evans.)

Maine, beautiful black and green cherts from Upstate New York, and, in rare instances, spectacular chert from Ramah Bay in northern Labrador, a thousand miles north of southern New Hampshire. Archaeologists can track the occurrence of these stones through time and across space, reflecting the waxing, waning, and redirection of long-distance social networks. They can then begin to ask questions to explain the patterns we see—and all this from non-descript chips of stone.

Following the Trail

One of the most enjoyable aspects of archaeology is that you never know where it's going to take you. In the same sort of dopamine release we experience when unwrapping a present, each shovelful of soil has the potential to show you something you haven't seen before, or something that will spark a question that, in turn, will lead to other questions and, before you know it, a full-blown research project.

That was my experience in my second summer of archaeology, working at the Eddy Site in Manchester, New Hampshire. Excavation of this deeply stratified site started with the removal of the fill deposited during the construction of Rt. 293. Once we were through this layer, we began excavating dark, flood-deposited soil, removing it in precise 3-cm-thick levels, and finding decorated ceramics and stone tools from the Late Woodland period, some 500 to 1,000 years before present. As we progressed deeper, we began finding small flakes of a beautiful, lustrous honey-colored stone, and a handful of small scraping and cutting tools of the same material. This stone was dramatically different from the typical quartz, rhyolite, or dusty weathered hornfels I was used to seeing, and when I asked, I was told it was Pennsylvania jasper, thought to come from quarries in southeastern Pennsylvania. In a few more 3-cm levels, this material disappeared and didn't show up again in any of the deeper, older deposits at the site.

I wondered why this material had travelled so far, and whether it was found on any other sites. I learned it had it also appeared on the other side of the Merrimack River at the Smyth Site, where a jasper Jack's Reef point, a finely made, corner-notched point dating to the second half of the Middle Woodland period 1,200–1,600 years ago, had been recovered, matching the age of the jasper at the Eddy Site.

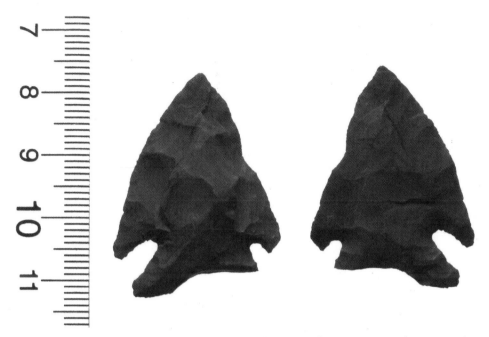

Figure 3.11. Broken jasper Jack's Reef point from Fryeburg, Maine, obverse and reverse views. From private landowner's collection. (Photograph by Arthur Spiess. Courtesy Maine Historic Preservation Commission.)

Two years later, in 1987, I returned to the question in my master's thesis, and began seriously combing through the archaeological reports for any occurrence of jasper in New England. This material did occur on other sites, and apart from a few Paleoindian sites, it was always in sites of the late-Middle Woodland period, where it was made into a variety of tools, including, most notably, Jack's Reef points. It only appeared as finished or nearly finished tools, indicating that New England was some distance from the original source. This stone was distributed from Cape Cod through eastern Massachusetts, New Hampshire, and all the way to the northern tip of Lake Champlain in Vermont. This beautiful stone was particularly abundant on coastal sites, most notably from around the salt marshes in Seabrook and Hampton, New Hampshire.

It was not just the raw material that arrived, but also the knowledge of how to use it. Jasper is a hard, brittle material, but when heated in a fire, fine microscopic cracks spread through the stone, making it easier to work. Heating also produces a chemical and visual change in the stone. Jasper's natural, yellow-brown color comes from a trace mineral, goethite, but heating transforms goethite into hematite, turning jasper a deep, rich red. Hematite is also the key component of red ocher, a substance used by Native people across North America as a base for paint and as a sacred inclusion in human burials. The jasper tools from New Hampshire sites all showed consistent evidence of heat-treating. Whether heating was used to improve workability, to achieve an aesthetic or even spiritual transformation of their tools by turning them blood-red, or both, is one of those many questions that are easy to pose and difficult to answer.

Archaeologists have long known that Native people had extensive social networks connecting people and cultures over considerable distances. While New England has been seen by some archaeologists as a backwater, the Native people here were full participants in these networks. Native people in western Vermont were buried with tubular tobacco pipes and beautifully made spear points made of stone from Ohio and copper artifacts from the Great Lakes, clearly linking them to the Adena culture, one of the earliest mound-building cultures in North America.

In the Midwest, the Adena culture is followed by the Hopewell culture, whose distinctive burial mounds were arranged in precisely surveyed patterns, and whose graves contained shells from the Gulf of Mexico, copper from the Great Lakes, mica from North Carolina, and obsidian from the Rocky Mountains. Hopewell-influenced mound building extended across most of eastern North America, and Hopewellian burial mounds were built in western New York, though none has ever been documented in New England.

Was this exotic jasper evidence that the people of northern New England were also part of this extensive network? It was an exciting idea, but the problem was that the dates were wrong. What some archaeologists have labeled the Hopewellian Interaction Sphere collapses by AD 400, right about the time jasper first appears on Middle Woodland sites in New England. It had to be something else, some separate phenomenon that was only just coming into focus. I learned that jasper Jack's Reef points weren't a strictly New England pattern, but occurred on sites as far away as western New York and Delaware. And to make things even more uncertain, a newly published scientific analysis comparing jasper artifacts with the jasper from Pennsylvania quarries showed that the Middle Woodland jaspers found in New England came not from these quarries but from a source unknown to modern geologists. I finished my thesis, described what I had discovered as a "Post-Hopewellian" network that would need more study, and moved on to a doctoral dissertation that would focus on ceramics.

More than two decades had gone by, each year marked by a vague resolution that I would return to my jasper research and get it published, when, in 2012,

I was invited to a symposium organized by a colleague in Michigan, who wanted to bring together archaeologists from across the northeast who had been studying Jack's Reef-related sites. Archaeologists with little or no prior acquaintance, working in areas as far flung as southern Quebec, Illinois, and Delaware had found the same pattern, with Jack's Reef points made of jasper and other exotic, high quality stone circulating throughout all of northeastern North America, dating to the same period as they did in New England. Once again, the Native people of New Hampshire were not isolated, but part of a vast network over which people exchanged ideas, spiritual beliefs, raw materials, and other elements of culture.

And then, after only a few centuries, by about AD 800, this material vanished from the archaeological record in New England as abruptly as if a spigot had been turned off. Did this mark the end of long-distance interaction? If so, why had it ended? There were other changes as well around this time, as across the northeast Jack's Reef points gave way to triangular Levanna points and the decorative patterns on ceramic pots changed. Also, for the first time, Native people in New England began growing corn, beans, and squash, domesticates from Central America that had spread across the continent, to supplement their traditional diet. Were these things connected? And if so, how? And was it really all about high-quality stone?

Years ago, archaeologist Barbara Leudtke urged her colleagues to focus on what may have been "going the other way" in exchange for jasper. This is a difficult question. Some of what may have been exchanged could have been perishable, things like beaver pelts or tobacco that leave no traces in the archaeological record. There may also not be a single answer to that question, as jasper almost certainly changed hands many times before being discarded as worn-out tools; in each one of these exchanges, different materials may have been given in return. Finally, it is likely that exchange was not really motivated by or centered on jasper. The notion of exchange as a purely economic endeavor, governed by the laws of formal economics such as supply and demand, is a product of modern capitalist societies. In non-stratified societies, exchange is about establishing and maintain social ties, and it is the strength and quality of these ties that shape interaction and the distribution of specific material goods, not the other way around. Archaeologists need to ask what led people throughout the Northeast to establish extensive social networks during this time, not why people wanted or needed high-quality stone.

Bones

Fire is a creator and a destroyer. For many years, anthropologists have argued that Native people would burn mature forests, whose tall trees and high canopies kept sunlight from the forest floor, to stimulate the growth of grasses, shrubs, and smaller trees. These in turn would increase the number of deer, making them a more reliable staple of the Native economy. These deer would be butchered, with some of the larger bones cracked to extract the fat-rich marrow. Some bones were used to make handles for stone tools, and others were thrown to the dogs, a constant presence around an Abenaki camp. The dogs would make short work of them, leaving little or nothing for the archaeologists to puzzle over. Even if they did manage to survive the dogs and the people, bones decay rapidly. However, if they wind up in a fire, bones become calcined, or chemically transformed, with the organic collagen burning off, leaving the mineral components, primarily calcium and phosphorous. These calcined bone fragments are resistant to decay, and, in an archaeologist's screen, appear as small chalky fragments, often with non-descript shapes, but sometimes with enough of the original form remaining so that, in the hands of an expert, the species and sometimes even the age of the animal can be identified.

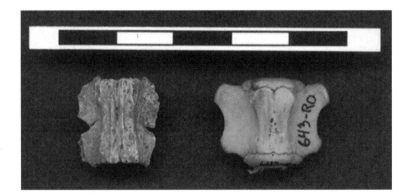

Figure 3.12. Left: calcined caudal vertebra from the tail of a beaver, site 27GR219, Holderness, New Hampshire, showing cut marks from a stone tool. Right: beaver caudal vertebra from Zooarchaeology Laboratory, Peabody Museum, Harvard University. The vertebra from Holderness was recovered in association with a 3,500-year-old stone tool. (Photograph by Tonya Largy.)

The ability to identify and interpret calcined bone from archaeological sites is a rare specialization. It requires extensive training in vertebrate anatomy to make the initial identifications, as well as access to a large comparative collection of animal skeletons. It also requires an understanding of the behavior and life cycles of different animals, knowing about seasonal migration patterns, hibernation, and when they birth and raise their young, information that can help determine the season of a site's occupation and provide other insights into Native life. It also requires an understanding of the archaeological record, so that the bones can be interpreted in relation to other artifacts they were found with, and the ability to see in them direct evidence of human activity, such as traces of cut marks, grinding, or polish reflecting butchering or tool manufacturing.

For more than two decades, I have worked with Tonya Largy, a zooarchaeologist on the staff of the Peabody Museum at Harvard University and one of only a handful of scientists specializing in analyzing bones from archaeological sites in New England. Along with having access to one of the world's best comparative collections of animal skeletons, Tonya has colleagues who are internationally recognized for their knowledge of particular types of animals, from turtles to snakes to small mammals to fish, and who can be consulted in the interpretation of particularly complex collections. In her hands, small fragments of calcined bone take on an identity. Sometimes they are so small and nondescript they can only be classified into general categories, like mammal, perhaps with a general size category (small, medium, large). Others, whose shapes are more complex and distinctive, can be identified to species, and distinctions can even be made between juveniles and adults.

Clay

I'm always hoping to find a fingerprint. On broken pieces of pottery, it's not unusual to see shallow, wide impressions on the inside of the pot, extending down from the rim, marking where an Abenaki woman had braced the wall of the wet clay pot with her fingers while striking the outside with a wooden paddle. If there was going to be a fingerprint preserved in clay, it would be there, at the end of the impression. A fingerprint, of course, wouldn't tell us anything we didn't already know—there'd be nothing to compare it to, and we already know Indian people have fingerprints. It would, however, focus our thoughts not on the object but on a person, the woman who crafted this pot and, in doing so, made dozens of individual choices, some responsive to the traditions of her people, learned from her mother, aunts, and grandmothers, and others of her own choosing, subtle innovations in decoration or form, that left a unique record for archaeologists to read.

Some of the earliest dated ceramics in the northeast have been found in New Hampshire, at sites on major waterfalls in Concord and Manchester radiocarbon dated to around 3,300 years ago. Like the stone tools whose styles were shared by people over vast areas, this early form of pottery is widespread, and the examples from western New York, southern Quebec, or New Jersey are hard to distinguish from the ones in Manchester. Known to archaeologists as Vinette I, after the site in New York where they were first found, these pots had thick, semi-conical bases and straight sides. They were not formally decorated, but both surfaces were covered with the rough impressions left by being struck with a textile or cord-wrapped wooden paddle. Like all Native pottery in the northeast before European contact, they were not painted or glazed, and they are occasionally encrusted around the rims with black, burned residue, most likely the remains of food.

Why did Native people begin making clay pots at this point in their history? As astute naturalists, they knew about this odd, sticky soil and where it could be found, and had seen it harden when it was caught in a passing forest fire. The question is why that knowledge was put to use when it was, and most archaeologists have assumed it had something to do with a change in the economy, and the growing importance of nuts, seeds, and other foods that were most nutritious if cooked for long periods of time. Whatever the answer, the need for permanent vessels for cooking or storage began at least seven hundred years earlier, when, across the northeast, people began making containers out of steatite, or soapstone. These steatite pots ranged in size from small cups to large cauldron-sized vessels, and the larger versions often had lug handles on the sides for carrying. They were almost never decorated, and the stone came from small, localized outcrops.

After five or six centuries, these pots were replaced by the first clay vessels. It may be that the small, local sources of steatite were played out, or that it took too many hours of laborious carving to create them. To the south of New England, in the Middle-Atlantic region, there is a direct transition, with the first clay pots made in the traditional shape of steatite bowls and with crushed pieces of steatite mixed in with the clay to give it added strength, almost as if the last stone pots were giving birth to this new technology, with the first potters acting as midwives.

A few observations by Europeans in the seventeenth century and the remembered traditions of Native peoples themselves, tell us that women were the potters in Native societies. Making ceramics was a regular and essential part of their work, and a basic mastery was something all women would likely acquire, although

Figure 3.13. Steatite pot, Wilkens Collection, central New Hampshire. (Photograph by Mark Greenly. Courtesy of the Mt. Kearsarge Indian Museum.)

some women, through experience, talent, or both, would have more skill than others. To make a pot, a woman would first find clay, perhaps in a small pocket in an eroding riverbank. She would mix small particles of crushed stone into the clay, or, if she lived near the coast, fragments of crushed clamshells. These additions are called temper and would provide a latticework of hard surfaces for the clay particles to adhere to, inhibiting cracking and increasing the pot's strength and durability.

Next, the clay would be rolled into thin coils and stacked up to form the basic shape of the pot. Each place where two coils met was a point of weakness, a place where future use might result in a crack or a catastrophic failure, so the potter spent considerable time bonding the coils together, repeatedly striking the vessel with a wooden paddle, and using her fingers or a smooth wooden or bone tool to meld the coils into a uniform wall. When this was done and the basic form of the pot was completed, she might apply decoration, usually just to the upper portion of the vessel. This decoration was created by stamping or incising the clay with a small, toothed implement, a smooth wooden stylus, or with the fabric or cord-wrapped edge of the wooden paddle she had used in the previous steps. By pressing, incising, or rocking the edge of her tool back and forth, she could create a variety of decorative patterns that would continue around the entire circumference of the upper portion of the vessel, the part that would be most visible. These decorations were meant to be seen, opening for archaeologists the possibility that they had meaning and were communicating messages about social or individual identity. This decoration had the added advantage of creating a roughened, irregular surface around the top of the pot, making it easier to lift and less likely to be dropped.

Once the decoration was complete, the pot was left to air-dry for a few days, and then fired in an open-air fire, placed upside down in the coals and covered with a thick layer of glowing embers. Potters refer to this technique as "low-firing"; it does not produce the high temperatures of a modern kiln and the resulting pot is softer, less durable, and more prone to absorb moisture. After a day or two, when the fire had died, the pots would be removed and be ready to use for cooking or storage, until when, months or years later, they would break and start to become part of the archaeological record. Only a handful of intact, complete pots have ever been found in New England. It is far more common to find a scatter of hundreds of small fragments, or sherds, from a single pot broken in use, broken again when stepped on or thrown into a trash pit, and broken further as the soil froze and thawed each winter for hundreds or thousands of years.

Making a stone tool is a subtractive process, which creates the final form by removing pieces, and where each step removes the traces of previous steps. Making a pot, in contrast, is an additive process, where the traces of the first steps—preparing the clay, adding temper, forming the vessel—are as visible to the archaeologist as the last steps of decoration and firing. In a single pot, then, you can see dozens of individual decisions, each determining a specific attribute of the pot, ranging from the kind of temper and how much is added, how large the temper fragments should be, how big the pot will be, what sort of tools to use in its decoration, and how those tools will be held and applied. Archaeologists can identify the decisions encoded in a single pot, comparing it to other pots from a single site or pots from a neighboring river drainage or region. The resulting patterns raise further questions, about how Native societies were organized, about shared practices and individual differences between groups or potters,

Figure 3.14. Reconstructed ceramic vessel, c. AD 400–800, Smyth Site, Manchester, New Hampshire. (Photograph by Mark Greenly. Courtesy of the Mt. Kearsarge Indian Museum and the Manchester Historic Association.)

and whether there were recognizable boundaries reflecting groups with their own shared ceramic traditions.

One of the first breakthroughs in using ceramics to understand social organization was by Victoria Bunker, who compared attributes of Middle Woodland pots in the Merrimack River drainage. In contrast to the river drainage model that suggested ceramics should be the same within drainages, she found differences between the northern and southern portions of the Merrimack in the first centuries of the Middle Woodland period, but saw these differences disappearing by the period's end. What this pattern meant, and whether it could be seen in other parts of the archaeological record, then became a direction for future research.

Ceramics can also reveal other types of technology we never see, particularly the tools that left their imprints on clay. We can recreate the size and shape of toothed, comb-like implements that were dragged or rocked across the surface of a pot by measuring the impressions and taking casts using soft modeling clay. We can also use potsherds to bring the textiles that almost never preserve in the archaeological record back to life. Pots retain the impressions of the last blows struck by a fabric-wrapped paddle, and when soft plasticine modeling clay is pressed into these impressions and then carefully pulled away, it can show a detailed, three-dimensional cast of the textile, with each cord and the individual fiber strands clearly visible.

But other than being a neat trick of conjuring up a missing piece of the puzzle, what do textile impressions tell us? In a masterful study completed in 1984, Jim Petersen and Nathan Hamilton compared the fabric impressions on early ceramics from northern New England. On pots that were otherwise indistinguishable, they found one attribute that divided them: how the natural fibers had been twisted. In making textiles, fibers must be twisted together to form the individual strands that will be woven together. These fibers can be twisted to the left or to the right, and there is no advantage to twisting in either direction. But this decision does produce a different pattern: a right twist leaves a *Z*-shaped pattern, and a left twist creates an *S*-shaped pattern. You can only see this if you

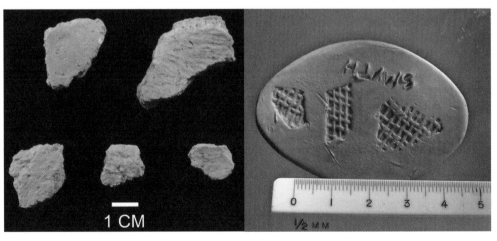

Figure 3.15. Ceramic sherds and plasticine impression revealing textiles, Smyth Site, Manchester, New Hampshire. (Courtesy of the New Hampshire Division of Historic Resources.)

look closely at a piece of cord, and you have to look even closer when it's the impression of a piece of cord on an ancient clay pot. It's not readily apparent to the naked eye, so it could not have been meant to be readily seen and was not one of those attributes that could have been intentionally used to communicate information about identity or anything else.

Figure 3.16. *S*– and *Z*–twists. (After Petersen and Hamilton 1984.)

When Petersen and Hamilton completed their analysis of sherds from dozens of sites across northern New England, a clear pattern emerged. Pots from sites along the coast were impressed with *Z*-twist textiles, and those from the interior were impressed with *S*-twist textiles. In every other respect, these pots were identical. Just as with Bunker's study in the Merrimack drainage, this pattern opens up other questions: Petersen and Hamilton argued that this reflected different "learning communities," with the implication being that there was some sort of boundary or difference between these two regions that kept at least this cultural choice separate and distinct for over a thousand years. Just like Bunker's Merrimack study that saw differences decline and disappear with time, this difference in one simple custom in textile production also disappears by the last centuries of the Woodland period. Why? In the archaeology of New England, questions produce a pattern that leads to yet other questions and patterns, resulting in some fitful, uneven movement towards a better understanding of the complexities of Native life and history.

For almost 3,000 years, ceramics across the northeast remain broadly similar. By AD 1500, however, right about the time of the first European contacts, ceramics begin to change dramatically. There is an elaboration in form, with round-bottomed or globular pots that have constricted necks, distinct collars, and, often, peaks or castellations along the rim. The pots are ornately decorated, most often with tightly spaced zones of incised decoration, small punctations made with the tip of a stylus, and even, on occasion, small human faces or effigies. These pots are

Figure 3.17. Colchester jar, Colchester, Vermont, showing elaboration in form and decoration. (Courtesy of the Fleming Museum of Art, University of Vermont.)

also made with a greater degree of skill than earlier pots, using very fine, uniform temper and having thinner walls that show little or no evidence of coil breakage.

The creative explosion in ceramics occurs across New England. An earlier generation of archaeologists, being familiar with the elaborately decorated, castellated pots made by Iroquoian people, argued that the styles were imported, with the Native women of New England imitating their more "advanced" neighbors to the west. The only problem with this argument is that there is no evidence these styles had occurred first among the Iroquois and only later spread east, nor is there any explanation for *why,* for example, Abenaki women would, at this time, want to imitate the forms of people linguistically and culturally so different from themselves.

Other archaeologists have argued that the elaborate styles of these pots are markers of tribal identity, but this argument also has problems. In southern New England, ceramic styles from this time period were used to conceal tribal differences, so that the products of Wampanoag, Mohegan, and Narragansett potters are essentially indistinguishable. In northern New England, distinct similarities between ceramics found on a handful of sites and those associated with the St. Lawrence Iroquois to the north have been noted, suggesting some degree of interaction, direct or indirect, between the Abenaki and the St. Lawrence Iroquois. What is less clear in northern New England is whether these styles contained meaning, communicating information about identity, spiritual beliefs, or other issues of concern to Native people, and if so, what this meaning or information was. We are still struggling to read these intricate and symbolically rich types of material culture.

CHAPTER 4
A Dam in the River

"**I** had to check you out first, you know," he said with a grin. And he had, calling his contacts in the ranks of professional archaeologists to ask if this new arrival in the Monadnock region was qualified and on the level. The speaker was avocational archaeologist, passionate outdoorsman, and life-long Swanzey resident, Arthur Whipple, who had spent a spring day in 2002 driving me around to Native American sites along the Ashuelot River, explaining how he had discovered them, what he thought about their potential, what the landowner's attitude might be toward possible excavation, and, in general, all the information I was looking for to get started doing archaeology in my new home area.

Unlike many scientific professions, archaeology has always had a large contingent of passionate amateur practitioners. Some of these were wealthy gentlemen pursuing grand theories, and many others were simply relic collectors, content to take their finds and use them, mounted with glue or wire on wooden boards, as decoration for the walls of their dens. In New England, these amateur, or avocational, archaeologists were responsible for amassing huge collections of artifacts, conducting some large-scale excavations, and forming state archaeological societies that coordinated their activities and published the results of their work. The best of these avocationals kept careful records of their discoveries, noting their locations and sharing the information with the few professionals interested in New England archaeology. Art Whipple was one of these. In the 1970s, he discovered one of the oldest sites in New England, a 12,000-year-old Paleoindian site in Swanzey on a high sandy bluff overlooking the Ashuelot River, bringing it to the attention of archaeologists from the University of Massachusetts-Amherst and working with them as they conducted a major excavation of the site, which they named in his honor. The Whipple Site quickly became one of the best known in northeastern North America.

Despite his accomplishments, Art would always downplay his considerable knowledge and defer to those with professional and academic training. But he had a deep understanding of the archaeology in this part of New Hampshire that came from his intimate familiarity with the environment gained through

Figure 4.1. Art Whipple at the Tenant Swamp Site, Keene, New Hampshire, 2010.
(Photograph by Robert Goodby.)

decades of hunting, fishing, and trapping. His love of nature gave him an insight into Native life that wasn't a part of any university training in anthropology. He was also a steward of the sites in the Monadnock region and would report any evidence of disturbance, vandalism, or looting to the proper authorities.

All the work I've done in the Monadnock region is built on the foundation Art laid down, even though his formal education ended with high school before he went off to serve in the army during the Korean War. When asked how I know where to look for sites, I typically talk about the importance of the environmental setting and how that made sense in a hunting and gathering economy. But for years, if the question came during a talk in the Monadnock region, I'd just smile and say, "Art Whipple tells me where they are."

One of the first sites Art took me to on that trip around the region in 2002 was the Swanzey Fish Dam. According to an account written in 1888 by George Wheelock: "Near by the old dam lives Jonas L. Moore. Here lived his father and grandfather before him. For one hundred and thirty years this has been called the Indian dam." This affirms that the dam was there when the first White settlers arrived in the mid-1700s, and that it was known to be part of the Native landscape.

To reach the dam, Art and I walked right over the Whipple Site, and then down a ravine and up the other side before reaching a high sandy terrace over-looking a sharp bend in the Ashuelot River. Continuing south, the terrace slopes gently downwards to where it is only a few feet above the level of river. We fought our way through the underbrush and stared at the deep, murky water. "That's where it is," Art said, "but you can't see it now."

Situated in what was originally a shallow, rocky, fast-moving stretch of the river, the Swanzey Fish Dam was made of the natural stones from the riverbed, which were rearranged to form a large, uneven "V" stretching across the river. It remained in plain sight until the 1860s, when a dam was built a few miles down-stream to power the Homestead Woolen Mill. This dam created an impoundment that changed the course of the river upstream, making it deeper and slower. The old Indian dam was covered, first with water, and then, over the years, with silt and eel grass, and became, for the most part, invisible. Only occasionally would a few of its stones come into sight before disappearing again, and it faded from memory as it did from view; one more piece of Native history lost to modern development.

The Indian dam made one brief reappearance in 1950, when the Woolen Mill Dam was temporarily dismantled for repairs and the Ashuelot dropped down to its natural level. Out of the silt, like a phoenix, the old dam reemerged, so dramatically visible that an airplane was sent up to take a photograph that appeared in a feature story in the *Keene Sentinel*. After a short time, though, the Woolen Mill Dam was replaced, the waters rose, and the dam again receded into memory. On the day Art showed me the site, only a few of the larger stones were visible, and I had to take it on faith that there was something down there waiting in the murky water.

If Native people were going to build something this dramatic, it made sense that it might be here, in the part of Swanzey known as Sawyer's Crossing. Local histories mentioned the abundance of Indian artifacts plowed up in the fields along the Ashuelot River (whose Abenaki name is *Azewald Zibo*), and some of the older life-long residents had amassed large collections. Local histories said that skeletons were also plowed up from time to time, and that on the east bank of the river one could see, at least in the late-nineteenth century, the earthen berm

Low Water Reveals Indian Dam On Ashuelot River In Swanzey

Figure 4.2. A 1950 *Keene Sentinel* article on the Swanzey Fish Dam. (Courtesy of the *Keene Sentinel*.)

Photo by Jack Teehan

INDIAN DAM. This aerial view shows a V-shaped dam built by the Indians on the Ashuelot river downstream from the covered bridge in Swanzey Center. Mentioned in the Swanzey town history, the dam is rarely exposed to view.

By JACK TEEHAN

A landmark of Indian culture in Cheshire county became visible once more this week when the old Indian dam on the Ashuelot river in Swanzey was exposed.

The stream level was lowered when gates were opened at the Homestead Woolen Mill dam in West Swanzey.

Seen only by a few county residents due to its remote location several hundred yards from the nearest highway, the V-shaped structure, almost hidden by eel grass is mentioned in the Swanzey town history and was built before the early settlers arrived.

Constructed with boulders, the dam points downstream in a long V. The stream is about 100 feet wide at that point.

The apex of the V is open and it is believed that it was a favorite Indian fishing spot. A flat boulder was located below the dam and was probably used as a platform for the spearing of salmon in the stream as they came through the opening in the dam.

A score of Indian fireplaces were ploughed up near the dam in the 19th century indicating that a tribal village was located in the area. River stones were used to build the fireplaces inside wigwams.

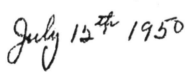

July 12th 1950

that was part of a fortification built by the Abenaki in early years of contact with the Europeans. Artifacts on display at the Swanzey Historical Museum showed the area had been occupied for many thousands of years, and data from the 12,000-year-old Whipple Site showed just how early that occupation had begun.

Additional evidence for the importance of Sawyer's Crossing to Indian people came from an intriguing map of Indian trails published in the 1960s, the work of New Hampshire historian Chester Price, an early member of the New Hampshire Archeological Society. Price had combed all the early histories of New Hampshire, gathering information, and compiled a map of the state showing an extensive network of linked trails and village locations. Many of these trails followed rivers, and others cut across the rugged landscape between drainage divides. The topography of New Hampshire makes travelling east-west a challenge, and these trails followed the easiest and quickest routes moving in this direction. A quick glance at Price's map shows that it bears an uncanny resemblance to a modern highway map, as these Indian trails were used by the first European settlers, who expanded them into cart paths, dirt roads, and eventually paved roads and the state's major highways. Anyone driving across New Hampshire today follows ancient routes laid down by the first inhabitants. Interestingly, on Price's map, five different trails come together at Sawyer's Crossing.

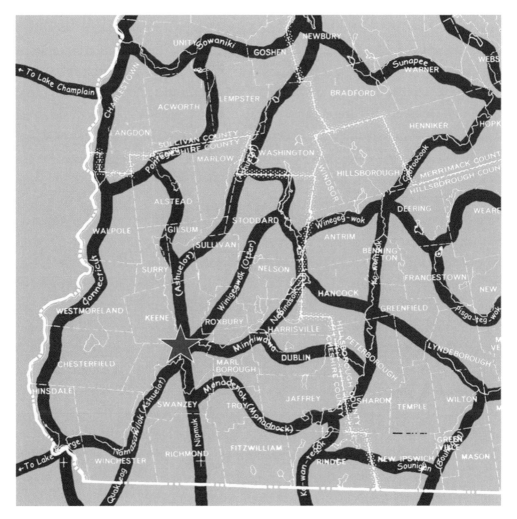

Figure 4.3. Chester Price Map of Indian trails showing convergence of trails at Sawyer's Crossing. (Courtesy of the New Hampshire Archeological Society.)

As suggestive as this all was, there was still a real question about the origin of the Swanzey Fish Dam. Nothing like this has been documented anywhere else in northern New England, and it was widely believed by archaeologists that Indians had not built substantial stone structures of any sort. Simon Griffin, who early on in his history of Keene had declared that very few Indians lived here, would devote two full pages to the Swanzey Fish Dam later in the same book, beginning with a declaration that "Indians were lazy, and this work of theirs was the more surprising on this account." There was also the practical problem of proving who built a structure made of unmodified stones, which themselves cannot be directly dated, and that were almost always under water and invisible.

The answer came, in part, from thinking about how such a dam would be used for fishing. The only thing that made sense was that it would have been used to catch the large schools of migratory fish that swarm the smaller tributaries of the Connecticut River in the spring and fall. While Griffin's fanciful description mentioned salmon, there is very little historical or archaeological evidence that significant numbers of salmon came up the Connecticut River. Instead, the most likely fish were members of the herring family, three of which—alewives, blue-backed-herring, and shad—are still plentiful today, swimming upstream every spring to their spawning grounds. These fish arrive in large, dense schools, and when encountering a V-shaped barrier in a shallow stretch of river would have been forced toward shore where they could be caught in large quantities with nets or baskets. In the fall, the pattern is reversed by the American eel, which migrates downstream and would have been neatly funneled into the point of the V.

What would people do after a successful day of fishing with hundreds of pounds of still-twitching fish? Native traditions and historical accounts say that fish would be dried on wooden racks above smokey fires, so they could be stored, preserved, and used in meals for months to come. It would make sense that this smoking would be done as close as possible to where the fish were caught. It stood to reason that the area immediately adjacent to the dam would have been a hive of activity, that we should find lots of artifacts reflecting this, and that the number of artifacts should decline the further away from the dam we went. Finally, there should be evidence of fires close to the dam. It was less likely that we would find any remains of the fish themselves, as their fine, cartilaginous bones would be unlikely to preserve, and because most historic accounts said that dried fish were cooked, bones and all, in stews with nuts, venison, corn, or whatever other foods were at hand, as witnessed first-hand by English colonial administrator Daniel Gookin in the seventeenth century:

> They frequently boil . . . fish and flesh of all sorts, either new-taken or dried, as shads, eels, alewives, or a kind of herring, or any other sort of fish. But they dry mostly those sort before mentioned. . . . these they cut in pieces, bones and all, and boil . . . they separate the bones from the fish in the eating thereof.

I decided to make this work the focus of my very first summer archaeological field school as a newly hired professor at Franklin Pierce College. My students and I would dig 50-cm-square shovel test pits placed at eight-meter intervals along both banks of the river, starting above the dam and continuing beyond it to the south. This method of excavating test pits is a common one used by archaeologists for locating sites. It bears a strong resemblance to the old game *Battleship*, where pegs are placed on a grid, and when there is a "hit," others are placed close around it to define the size, shape, and nature of what has been encountered. Like the pegs in *Battleship*, the odds are also good that most of your shovel test pits will come up empty.

The landowners on both sides of the river had given us permission to do the work, so the field school was scheduled for June of 2002, with fifteen enthusiastic student archaeologists, none of whom had ever excavated a site. I didn't get much sleep the night before field school started. While I had reason to think we *might* find Native artifacts, it wasn't certain they would be there, and I had visions of digging for days, and then weeks, finding nothing, and trying to convince an increasingly disappointed and disgruntled group of students that knowing the Indians *didn't* build the (invisible) dam was also significant. This scenario played over and over in my head that night, culminating with them all demanding a refund for their tuition and changing their majors to Business Administration. But by 10:30 the next morning we were in the field, on the high terrace well north of the dam, and our very first test pit produced Indian artifacts: flakes of rhyolite left over from an episode of toolmaking.

Extending out test pits hundreds of feet south, getting ever closer to the dam, we documented a patchwork scatter of artifacts, most of them reflecting brief episodes of tool making, and the base of a broken Neville point, a style dated between 7,000 and 8,000 years before present. Occasionally, half-finished tools were recovered, many of them strangely misshapen and marked by the steep-edged step fractures that are the mistakes of a novice flintknapper, perhaps from a long-ago afternoon when a grandparent patiently oversaw the earnest efforts of

Figure 4.4. Decorated ceramic rim sherds from the Swanzey Fish Dam, c. AD 1500–1700. (Photograph by Mark Corliss.)

a beloved grandchild. But as the terrain dropped down and the edge of the river and the dam got closer, the artifacts began to change.

After getting two teams of students set up by the dam location with their screens, shovels, and paperwork, I made a quick trip back up the terrace to help the rest finish up. When I returned to the dam a few minutes later, the students were looking at me excitedly, and one of them extended a hand, placing in my palm an intricately decorated, thin-walled piece of Native American pottery, typical of the period around first European contact. Soon, more of this pottery was emerging, including some undecorated sherds from the main body of the vessels that were the thinnest I had ever seen: at 2–3-mm, they were barely thicker than a fine porcelain teacup, and obviously the work of master potters.

By now, the rest of the students had joined us at the dam, and the number and variety of artifacts increased rapidly. A few hours after the discovery of the first ceramics, the broken half of a ground-stone gouge was recovered, and shortly thereafter, the first of four large, broad-bladed stone tools. Known as Atlantic points, they are dated to a narrow period of a few centuries toward the end of the Archaic period, between 4,100 and 3,800 years ago. Because of their large size and often asymmetrical shape, resulting from repeated resharpening of the

Figure 4.5. Stone tools recovered adjacent to the Swanzey Fish Dam; Atlantic points on bottom row. (Photograph by Steve Bayly.)

lateral margins, archaeologists believe these were cutting and processing tools, with at least one arguing they were specialized tools for processing fish. Three other points, stylistically dated between 2,000 and 4,000 years before present, were also recovered over the course of the next few seasons of work at the site.

So far, the hypothesis that Native people had built the dam was holding up. Right by the dam was a greater quantity and variety of artifacts than we had found anywhere else, including likely fish-processing tools, indicating that the reported location of the dam was indeed where people's efforts were focused. This was apparent even though the area by the dam, like so many Native sites, was not pristine but had been subjected to a century or two of plowing and the collection of artifacts by local residents. The extent of this disturbance is suggested by Wheelock's account of the dam. Referring to the family that owned it, he wrote: "The elder Moore dug up a half peck of arrow and spearheads, all in one pocket . . . Some twenty Indian fire-places have been ploughed up here." So clearly, what we were recovering was only a remnant of what had once been a much richer site.

Even with this disturbance, we were finding valuable information about the age of the dam. All that was missing was evidence of fire, but that too would come, in the form of three hearths made of densely-packed river cobbles, reddened and cracked by high heat. While the tops of these hearths had been disturbed by years of plowing, the remainder was intact, and two of these yielded small pieces of burned wood, recovered between the pieces of reddened stone, that were submitted for radiocarbon dating. Both dates were essentially the same, one spanning between 3,480 and 3,900 years before present, and the second between 3,635 and 4,155 years before present—both consistent with the stylistic age of the stone tools. So, the dam *was* built by Native Americans, the first use of the dam occurred around 4,000 years ago, and the thin-walled decorated pottery showed its use had continued up until the time of European contact, explaining how the first settlers knew it was an Indian dam.

As if to help make the picture complete, in 2010 the Homestead Woolen Mill Dam was removed again, this time for good, part of an effort to restore migratory fish populations in the Ashuelot. Just as in 1950, the water level at the

Figure 4.6. Swanzey Fish Dam, view east, November 2012. (Photograph by Garrett Evans.)

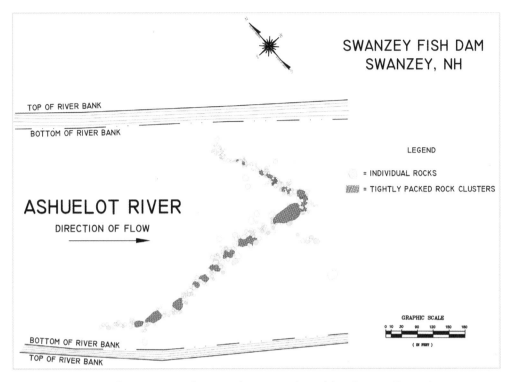

Figure 4.7. Map of Swanzey Fish Dam. (Map produced by Garrett Evans.)

fish dam dropped, the water ran more swiftly, the silt was washed away, and the old Indian dam rose again, there for all to see, stubbornly asserting that Native people had indeed been here. This also provided the chance to create a detailed map of the entire dam, so on a cold day in late November of 2012, with my surveyor-archaeologist friend Garrett Evans, we mapped the stones of the dam using a total station, Garrett high and dry on the bank using the sophisticated surveying instrument, and me, less skilled, in the frigid water with high rubber boots, holding the prism pole on every sizeable stone I could see. The result was a clear picture of the entire dam; rather than a *V*, it looked more like a giant check-mark, creating a barrier that would have forced migrating fish to the banks in the spring and confined eels in the apex in the fall. The dam took advantage of several large naturally occurring boulders in the riverbed, connecting them with walls of smaller boulders and river cobbles to form a barrier that extended from one bank to the next.

By 2012, after ten years of episodic work, the question of the Swanzey Fish Dam had been answered. It was built by Native Americans, dating back at least 4,000 years, showing that Native Americans in New England could and did build substantial structures out of stone. Nor was it unique. In 2004, Franklin Pierce student Quinn Ogden (who would go on to a career as a professional archaeologist) completed a senior thesis showing that *V*-shaped dams are in fact well-documented across much of eastern North America, but just hadn't been seen in New England. Once again, the Native inhabitants of the Monadnock region were not isolated but integrated into a network of shared traditions that extended for thousands of miles.

As important as the findings about the dam were, though, there was something even more important that emerged from this work. Putting together all the historical records, the collections by amateur archaeologists, Price's map, and the work at the Whipple and Swanzey Fish Dam sites, it was apparent that the area around Sawyer's Crossing had been occupied continuously by Native people for more than 12,000 years. Rather than being a transitory stop for nomadic people, this was a central place, lived in and returned to for more than 400 generations. Its permanence was different than that understood by the White settlers; instead

Figure 4.8. Franklin Pierce University archaeology students, 2013 excavations at the Swanzey Fish Dam. Field Assistant Gail Golec, kneeling on left; Robert Goodby, standing in rear. (Photograph by Robert Goodby.)

of living here year-round, the Native people returned every season for an immense span of years. Families gathered there, children were born, people died and were buried, making it a sacred place as well as a place to fish. The first people arrived when the last of the mammoths and mastodons were dying off, and they were still here when the Europeans came, choosing this location to build a fort as their hold on their ancient homeland grew uncertain. It is this continuity, this deep sense of time and place, that is shown by all the archaeological work. Although the memories of this place may have faded or disappeared and its Abenaki name become lost in the bloody history of the last few centuries, the fact of that continuity remains.

CHAPTER 5

A Knoll in the Forest

Figure 5.1. Work beginning at the Raft Bridge Site, June 2007. (Photograph by Robert Goodby.)

On the first day of field school in the summer of 2007, my students clambered out of our van at a camp in Hancock, New Hampshire, shouldered the equipment, and began a fifteen-minute walk into the woods, along a rutted trail that took them to a small, level knoll overlooking wetlands to the east and the slow-moving waters of Nubanusit Brook, a tributary of the Contoocook River, to the west. Fifteen years before, a brief archaeological survey commissioned by the US Army Corps of Engineers had discovered a tiny handful of quartz flakes, enough to say that Native people had been here. They had also given it a name, the Raft Bridge Site, after a nearby rope-and-raft bridge used by campers to cross the

Nubanusit. But was there more to the Raft Bridge Site than a momentary episode of tool-sharpening?

Before we started work, I charged my students with answering questions of time and space that are central to archaeology and apply to all sites: How many times was the site occupied? How old are the different occupations? What is the size of the site and where are its boundaries? What sorts of activities took place? And finally, during which season of the year was it occupied? If these questions could be answered, then, later in the process, we could ask how a site is related to other sites used by the same people during their annual travels.

Archaeologists, of course, love to sort things into types, and just as we do with stone tools or decorated potsherds, we do this with sites. Habitation sites are places where a number (perhaps dozens) of families lived for days, weeks, maybe for as long as a season. This type of site should have a large number and wide variety of artifacts, as well as the remains of cooking hearths, storage pits, and other specialized features. A habitation site is likely to have a specific area where refuse is disposed, to keep it from accumulating where people are sleeping or preparing food. In contrast, a site left by an overnight trip by three or four hunters will be small, with the remains of a single small fire and only a few artifacts (a few pieces of burned animal bone, some flakes from tool sharpening, the broken bases of a spear point, a few rough, large stone tools used for butchering) discarded where they were used.

What kind of site was Raft Bridge? We knew almost nothing about the site, not even the exact location of the original finds, but we did know it was a wonderful setting for people who were hunting and gathering. It was situated in an ecotone, an area where different environmental zones converge, and the people who had worked on this knoll would have had ready access to all the resources of the forest, the stream, and the wetlands. We laid out our test pits and began excavating, and soon began finding small quantities of artifacts distributed across the knoll, sometimes in discrete clusters representing single moments in time. A cluster of tiny hornfels flakes on the north end of the knoll showed where a tool had been sharpened. A cluster of burned bone, later identified as turtle and beaver, was found at the southern end. A few small fragments of pottery were scattered across the knoll, two of them showing the impressions of S-twist fabric on the interior and exterior surfaces, dating them to between 2,000 and 3,300 years before present.

Near the top of the knoll, our excavations exposed a bowl-shaped concentration of charcoal: the remnants of an old cooking hearth. Soil in and around

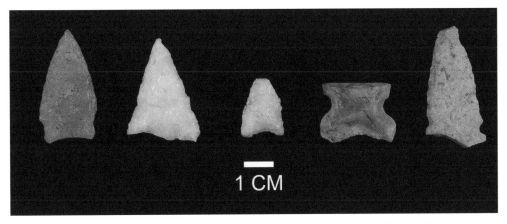

Figure 5.2. Stylistically distinct stone tools, Raft Bridge Site. Meadowood point is on the far right. (Photograph by Steve Bayly.)

the hearth contained twenty-two fragments of burned turtle bone, the smashed remnants of a quartz cobble from a brief episode of tool making, and a quartz scraping tool. Radiocarbon dating of wood charcoal from the hearth put its age between 5,800 and 6,200 years before present, clearly older than the pottery, showing the site had been occupied at least twice.

Five stylistically distinct stone tools were found. The styles of three of these dated between 4,000 and 6,000 years ago, consistent with the radiocarbon date of the hearth. One of these was a thin, exquisitely crafted tool made of high-quality Cheshire quartzite from central Vermont, and a second was the base of a broken point made of an exotic grey-black chert. A fourth tool, a small, triangular quartz point, dated between 2,000 and 5,000 years ago, and a fifth point, a delicately notched Meadowood point, dated to the Early Woodland period, between 2,000 and 3,300 years ago, matching the age of the fabric-impressed ceramics.

Putting everything together, the site was visited at least twice, once around 6,000 years ago, and again between 3,300 and 2,000 years ago, and was probably occupied more often than that. The small number of artifacts and the fact that they were still visible in discrete clusters indicated that these visits had been short and were made by relatively few people. More insight would come from the 232 small fragments of burned bone studied by Tonya Largy and turtle expert Joseph Martinez of the Harvard Museum of Natural History. Eight beaver bones were recovered from the south-central part of the knoll, including a fragment of an ulna (forearm) from a juvenile animal. One hundred and twelve bones were identified as turtle, including fragments from the shells of three very distinct species: painted turtles, snapping turtle, and the eastern box turtle. Beaver and turtle bone were found in close proximity in the southern part of the site, and, in one instance, shell fragments from a snapping turtle and a painted turtle were found in direct association, showing that turtle hunting was a coordinated, important activity. These bones also established the season the site was occupied. Both beaver and turtles are most active in the warm weather months, and turtles, who hibernate underground or burrow into the muddy banks of a stream, are almost inaccessible in the winter. So, the Raft Bridge Site was used in the warm part of the year, when small groups of people would come, perhaps for a day or an afternoon, the adults tending traps and gathering edible and medicinal plants from the wetlands while the children, in an activity both fun and helpful, scoured the stream and marshes for turtles.

But where, if this picture is accurate, did these people live, where did they return once night was falling and their tasks were complete? Did they walk to a

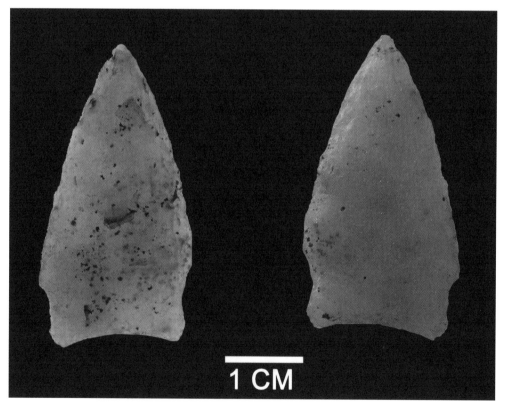

Figure 5.3. Close-up obverse and reverse view of a Cheshire quartzite projectile point. (Photograph by Steve Bayly.)

location a mile away or get in canoes to travel miles downstream? And if they were in this area in the summer, where did they go in the fall to hunt deer and gather nuts, and where did they spend their winters? These sites have yet to be discovered. At least one of them may have been around the low-lying terrain at the confluence of the Nubanusit and the Contoocook Rivers, which is now covered with asphalt and concrete in downtown Peterborough. For now, the Raft Bridge Site is a piece of the puzzle floating in time and space, waiting for us to find other sites to connect it to.

CHAPTER 6

The Snakes of Wantastiquet

Figure 6.1. The Wantastiquet Mountain Site, summer 2004, showing the eroding bank. (Photograph by Robert Goodby.)

A low creaking sound was all the warning we had, as a sixty-foot-high tree clinging to the edge of the riverbank started a slow-motion lean before suddenly accelerating and taking its entire root system down the fragile, eroding sandy slope and into the Connecticut River. Soil full of Native American artifacts rolled down the slope in its wake, and one more piece of this ancient site was taken by the river. The bank was now only a foot or so from the closest excavation unit, and the archaeologists quickened their pace.

An archaeological career is full of reluctant, painful farewells, when you come to the last day at a site, knowing there are still artifacts there and more that could be done, but you have to walk away because you're out of time or money, abandoning it to the bulldozers or the unyielding forces of nature. In the summer of 1985, on our last day at the Eddy Site in Manchester, I was full of angst, knowing we hadn't recovered everything that was there, and that there was no law that would protect what was left. As we drove away, the director, Victoria Bunker, shook her head and said, "You can't think like that. Never look back. Just go on to the next one." That proved to be an important lesson, in part because more and more sites are disappearing before our eyes. The Wantastiquet Mountain Site was one of these.

It was 2004, and after a few years working at the Swanzey Fish Dam, I was looking for a new field school site, and turned once again to Art Whipple. He took me to the bank of the Connecticut River in the very southwestern corner of the state, and showed me a narrow, level terrace with an eroding edge that dropped almost vertically down to the river and a few stone tools and pieces of pottery he'd found there over the years. The terrace was an unlikely spot for a habitation site, a narrow strip of land pinned between the river and the rocky foot of Wantastiquet Mountain (*Wantastegok Wadso*, in Abenaki). But like the Swanzey Fish Dam, it hadn't always been this way, and much of what had once been was gone.

Historic maps are one of the tools archaeologists use to understand the setting of Native American sites. While not concerned with the landscape or geography of Native people, these maps show how the land has changed over the past few centuries, how rivers have meandered, where old roads and railroads used to be, and how dams have changed the shorelines of lakes and ponds or the courses of rivers. The historic maps for the area around Wantastiquet Mountain told a story that explained why Art had found a site here, and what that site might have looked like. Nineteenth-century maps showed two large islands in the river directly west of Wantastiquet Mountain, the northernmost of which carried the roadway connecting Hinsdale, New Hampshire, and Brattleboro, Vermont. By the time the US Geological Service produced its 1935 topographic map, however, the Vernon hydroelectric dam had been built downstream; the southern island had completely disappeared, and the northern island was less than half its original size. By the late-twentieth century, all that was left was a stone-reinforced remnant carrying the bridge. Soil survey maps showed the soil of the remaining island was identical to that of the site on the eroding terrace, but different from the soil on the Vermont side, indicating that these islands were once part of an expansive terrace extending into the river from the New Hampshire side, and that the eroding terrace was all that remained of this once-extensive landform.

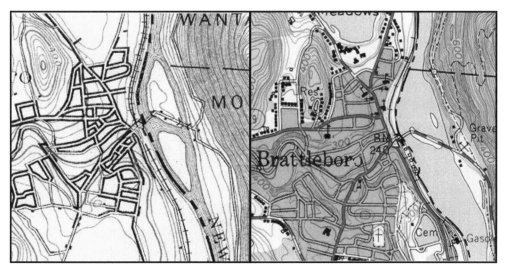

Figure 6.2. Historic topographic maps from 1893 (left) and 1954 (right) showing erosion of a large island that was originally an alluvial terrace on the east bank of the Connecticut River

This terrace would have been an ideal place for Native people to live. It was situated at the equivalent of a modern highway juncture, with the West River (*Wantastekw*, in Abenaki) joining the Connecticut less than a mile to the north, providing access to the interior of Vermont. A few miles downriver, the Ashuelot empties into the Connecticut, providing a route to Swanzey and points further north and east. The soil was well-drained and sandy, so it would have stayed dry even after a heavy rain. But the most unusual attraction would be found on the rocky slopes and summit of Wantastiquet Mountain.

Our goal in this excavation was simple: to save as much as we could of the site before the next spring flood. Test pits were used to confirm the presence of a rich, deep site along the terrace, and show that the site ended just before the rocky toe of the mountain slope. Larger excavation blocks were then used to recover the remains of cooking hearths and concentrations of artifacts. This was one of those deep, stratified sites on a river flood plain, with distinct layers of artifacts extended almost three feet below surface, where change and continuity over time could be studied in a controlled setting. Work at the site continued for the next two summers, and in 2005 the Franklin Pierce crew was joined by volunteers from the New Hampshire Division of Historical Resources SCRAP program.

This was a rich site. Thousands of flakes, most of high-quality Cheshire quartzite from central Vermont, showed that toolmaking was an important activity. Other evidence for toolmaking included a small cache of three quartzite preforms, reflecting the first stage of manufacture when stone is roughly shaped. A stone axe spoke of heavy woodworking. Flaked stone tools stylistically dated between 500 and 5,000 years before present were recovered, and they were arrayed in perfect chronological order, with the most recent styles closest to the surface and the oldest coming from as deep as three feet. Over seven hundred fragments of pottery from at least fifteen different vessels came from the uppermost layers of soil, bearing complex stamped designs from the Middle and Late Woodland periods, between 2,000 and 500 years before present.

The remains of stone hearths were also recovered, surrounded by artifacts and small fragments of burned bone, including one perfectly preserved circular hearth found in the lowest, oldest occupation level. Radiocarbon dates from four of these hearths confirmed the age of the site's occupations. A hearth 30 cm below surface was dated between 540 and 740 years before present, two hearths between 40 and 50 cm below surface produced dates from 930 to 1,290 and 1,280 to 1,600 years before present, respectively, and the deeply buried circular hearth, 75 cm below surface, was dated between 4,850 and 5,290 years before present.

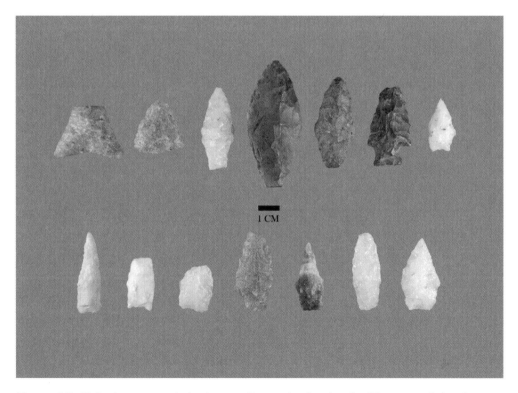

Figure 6.3. Flaked stone tools in descending order by depth. (Photograph by Garrett Evans.)

Figure 6.4. Decorated ceramic sherds dating between 2,000 and 500 years before present. (Photograph by Garrett Evans.)

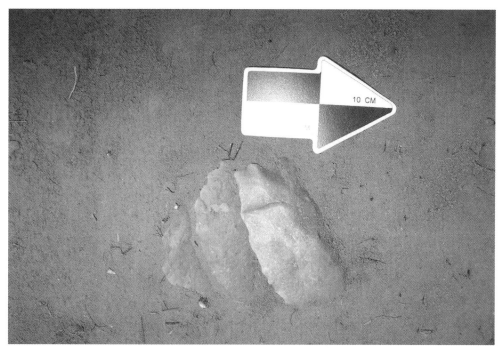

Figure 6.5. A cache of three roughly shaped Cheshire quartzite preforms. (Photograph by Robert Goodby.)

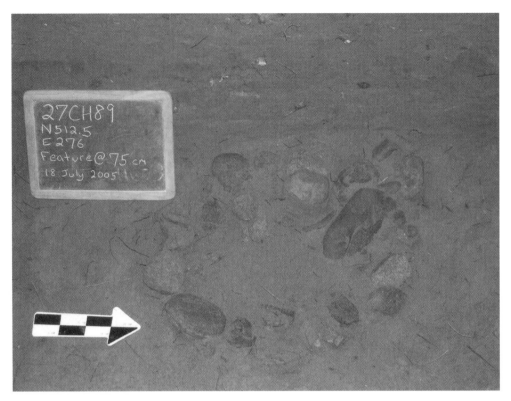

Figure 6.6. Circular stone hearth radiocarbon-dated between 4,850 and 5,290 years before present. (Photograph by Robert Goodby.)

Before we were done with the second week of excavation, we had noticed another pattern. This site was producing some very interesting pieces of calcined bone, not just from the hearths, but from across the site and in every layer of soil. What made these bones interesting was their shape. They were not the typical, non-descript fragments of mammal long bone or turtle shell, but were clearly the vertebrae of some small animal. One of my field assistants, Gail Golec, had advanced training in osteology and vertebrate anatomy, and after examining a number of them on site, shrugged her shoulders and said, "I think they're snakes."

At the end of each of our two seasons at Wantastiquet Mountain, we shipped the bones to Tonya Largy for identification and analysis. Tonya agreed with Gail that most of our bone was snake and enlisted the aid of her Harvard colleague Dr. Van Wallach, an international authority on snakes, to make more precise identifications, which he was able to do for twenty-five of the vertebrae. He determined that one was from a northern water snake, a second from a common garter snake, and two were from black rat snakes. Then things got really interesting. Another vertebra was identified as coming from the venomous northern copperhead, and

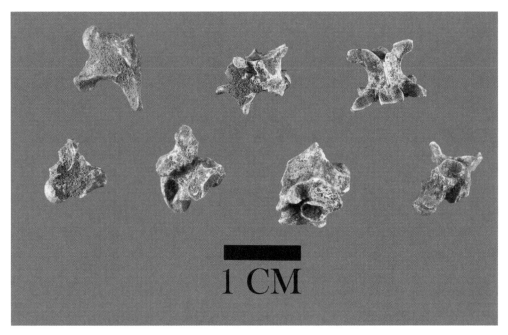

Figure 6.7. Timber rattlesnake vertebra, Wantastiquet Mountain Site. (Photograph by Mark Greenly and Garrett Evans.)

the remaining twenty vertebrae were from the equally dangerous timber rattlesnake. These timber rattlesnake bones were not from a single snake—they came from all levels of our excavation, with the deepest vertebra coming from 97 cm below surface, even deeper than the 5,000-year-old circular hearth.

What were people doing with deadly snakes for over 5,000 years? There's abundant evidence that snakes, including rattlesnakes, were eaten by Native Americans. But rattlesnakes are also an important animal to many Native American cultures, appearing in sacred art and being held in high regard, honored with titles like "grandfather." In northwestern Vermont, a Native American cemetery dating between 2,000 and 3,200 years ago included the burial of a middle-age man interred with a leather "medicine" bag containing the articulated skeletons of a timber rattlesnake and black rat snake, along with bones of pine marten, mink, fox, raccoon, and duck. In an 1884 Abenaki-English language book compiled by Abenaki elder Joseph Laurent, the Abenaki word for rattlesnake is *sisikwa*, and they were important enough to be included in the selective vocabulary the book provides.

Wantastiquet Mountain has been a notorious haven for rattlesnakes since the time of European contact. An 1883 article in the *Brattleboro Reformer* stated that:

> Wantastiquet mountain [is] . . . known by those living on the New Hampshire side as the "rattle-snake den." Andrew D Thomas accidentally discovered the haunts of these venomous serpents and he thus describes his experience: " . . . we had mowed out six rattlers from our hayfield which were stiff and dormant from the effects of the early morning cold. Thinking perhaps we might possibly run upon more we armed ourselves with heavy canes and sauntered out. After walking about the mountain we came across a hole in the ground a trifle smaller than that of a wood-chuck. By thrusting our sticks down into it we soon discovered that it was inhabited by snakes, and immediately after we were startled by seeing them all about us, hundreds of them seemingly, coiled on the ground, on stumps, and in fact, up in the bushes."

About this time, the rattlesnakes were so abundant that they began to be hunted commercially, and an 1886 article from the *Reformer* described how:

> Two more rattlesnakes have been killed the past week. The first was killed by Miss Mary Howe, as she was coming over the mountain. The other was killed by Andrew Horton, the veteran rattlesnake killer, who has already killed over 200 of them. Mr. Horton says he frequently catches the snakes alive, and has sold some of them for over ten dollars apiece.

Almost 140 years after these descriptions, Wantastiquet Mountain is one of the last remaining habitats for the endangered timber rattlesnake in New Hampshire. More research on the behavior and habits of snakes also helped explain why the bones of so many different species were used at Wantastiquet. While they are distinct species and unable to reproduce with each other, timber rattlesnakes, northern copperheads, and black rat snakes all share dens during hibernation and could have been encountered by anyone climbing to the summit in search of snakes.

But were the snake remains at Wantastiquet sacred or secular, the remains of a quick meal or the relics of a ritual act incorporating one of the most respected animal spirits in Abenaki cosmology? Even asking this question draws a line between the sacred and secular that might not have been recognized by the people at Wantastiquet. It also assumes that they couldn't be both, depending on the context. Like the difference between a table wine on Saturday night and the contents of a chalice on Sunday morning, the line isn't in the food itself but in the context it is consumed. And most of the context for the Wantastiquet rattlesnakes had long since been swept away by the dark waters of the Connecticut River.

On one of my last days at Wantastiquet, I was working alone, finishing up some mapping and taking a few final photographs. When I was done, I stood on the narrow terrace, looking down at the erosion and out into the wide waters of the Connecticut River, picturing a site that had covered thousands of square feet where a busy community lived on a broad terrace dotted with bark-covered wigwams, where the sun rose over Wantastiquet Mountain each morning, waking the snakes with its warmth as it woke the people with its light. Canoes were tethered along the river, ready to set out for points north and south, and the barking of dogs and the sounds of children carried over the broad plain. All of this had disappeared, gone long before Art Whipple had brought me here, and there was no retrieving it. All that was left was this little sliver of terrace, and soon that too would be gone, swept away by the river and time. But maybe it was this edge of the puzzle that was the most interesting piece of all—maybe it was here that a small party had paused and, led by an elder, a shaman respected for their wisdom, shared a quiet prayer before heading up *Wantastegok Wadso* to hunt for sisikwa. Maybe it was here that they paused when they returned, to offer thanks, and to carefully prepare what they had killed for a meal more to nourish the soul than the body. The small pieces of bone we pulled from our screens would never answer this question, but leaving it unasked, in the light of all we know about Native beliefs and traditions, would be a disservice to the place and the people who lived there.

75

CHAPTER 7

Where it All Began

I parked by a long-abandoned Little League baseball field and walked south into the woods. It was quiet and serene, on a level terrace deeply shaded by tall pines overlooking a vast wetland. Standing there in November of 2009, it was hard to imagine that this would soon be a bustling, modern middle-school campus with over six hundred students, and it definitely didn't occur to me that I was standing on one of the most significant Native American sites in New Hampshire.

I was there as an archaeological consultant, hired by the local school district, SAU 29, to assess whether there might be any significant archaeological sites on the property. Most people, if they think about where archaeologists work, would place them in museums or universities, but for the past fifty years, most professional archaeologists have made a living doing what I was doing: helping clients comply with the requirements of the National Historic Preservation Act. The Act, signed into law in 1966 in an era when federal highway and urban renewal projects were destroying historic neighborhoods, Civil War battlefields, and archaeological sites, sought to contain this damage by requiring any *federal* undertaking to take into account the effect of the project on significant historic sites. Significant, in this case, meant being eligible for inclusion on the National Register of Historic Places, a high standard that the vast majority of sites don't meet. But what did this have to do with a middle school in southwestern New Hampshire?

Keene, New Hampshire, is the only city in Cheshire County, and for years it has had a regional middle school and high school that serve the people of Keene and more than half a dozen surrounding communities. My daughter had attended the old Keene Middle School, located in the center of Keene in a decrepit brick cavern built almost a century earlier, lacking modern classrooms, adequate parking, proper athletic facilities, and most of the other features of a modern school. The region desperately needed a new school, and a location was chosen two miles northwest of the city center on a parcel of land bordered by two roads, an elementary school, and the sprawling five hundred acres of Tenant Swamp, a large wetland drained by the Ashuelot River. This was to be the site of a state-of-the-art school costing over thirty-eight million dollars. Architects were hired, bonds were issued, and a target opening of September 2011 was announced. The design for the campus, completed by Marinace Architects, would utilize every square foot of available space and include modern athletic fields between the main school buildings and Tenant Swamp. But building this close to a wetland would require a permit, and that's where an archaeological study, not anticipated in the original plan, would come in.

To build next to a wetland in New Hampshire, you need a permit from the New Hampshire Department of Environmental Services, which acts as a proxy for the US Army Corps of Engineers, who were given jurisdiction over the nation's waterways shortly after the founding of the republic. Since the modern definition of waterways includes wetlands and groundwater, that made the Keene Middle School project a federal undertaking, kicking off the National Historic Preservation Act review process. I got a phone call in October 2009, asking me to conduct the initial study.

This first phase of work is where most projects begin and end. The goal is to determine if there are any sites known or likely to be affected by a proposed project, and in 90% of cases, the answer is no. It includes research, looking at the project's environmental setting, archaeological site files maintained by the New Hampshire Division of Historical Resources, and town histories and historic maps. The research is followed by a systematic inspection of the site, looking for evidence of old cellar holes, forgotten family cemeteries, or perhaps Indian artifacts scattered around the entrance to a woodchuck burrow or in the upturned roots of a fallen tree. I already knew there were no recorded Native American sites in the vicinity, and the historic maps didn't show any residences until well into the twentieth century, only noting that local mill owner John Colony had killed a bear here sometime before 1877. My inspection of the site didn't reveal any evidence of historic occupation, not so much as a stone wall or a dirt road. The only evidence of human activity I found was recent, a small area where some homeless people had camped. Other than this, it looked untouched.

Standing there on that November day, I got a sense that there might be a Native American site here. Long-time archaeologists joke about how some places make their senses tingle, and this was one of those places. It was on level terrain on a high terrace, and the adjacent wetland was the traditional Native equivalent of a Wal-Mart, chock full of plants used for food and medicine, birds, turtles, snakes, aquatic mammals like beaver and otter, and other animals coming to drink and eat. The terrace was an ideal spot to be, with a southern exposure that would keep it relatively warm, and from where they could look out over the wetlands and watch the movement of game. It was also underlain by bone-dry sand that didn't hold water even after a heavy rain, making it unsuited for cultivation by the eighteenth- and nineteenth-century farmers of Keene, but ensuring Native inhabitants would never live on wet soil. To test my hunch, I would need to put some shovels in the ground.

I sent the report of my findings to Bill Gurney, superintendent of SAU 29, a few days later with the recommendation to excavate shovel test pits along the edge of the terrace overlooking the wetland. Amid this enormous, complex building project this recommendation from the archaeologist was a minor detail. The school was supposed to be open in twenty-two months, ground hadn't even been broken, and the clock was ticking. I was asked for assurances that the work could be completed quickly and given the go-ahead.

Working with a small crew of experienced archaeologists, we laid out ninety-two test pits on an eight-meter grid. Winter was coming, and we were delayed by a cold snap that left the soil frozen, but this gave way to a warm spell and the work proceeded quickly as the fine, dry sand was easy to dig and even easier to screen, not only because the soil fell right through the mesh, but because there were no artifacts to collect. This work is typically done by two-person teams, but on November 19, a crew of only three people meant that one person would dig alone, and that person was me. I filled my screen, picked it up off the ground, shook it a few times, and was surprised to see a few small flakes of a grey-tan rhyolite and a lustrous reddish-brown chert. A few more shovels of soil brought the total number of flakes to forty-five.

One of my crew members that day was Yvonne Benney Basque, who had years of experience working with New Hampshire State Archaeologist Richard (Dick) Boisvert on sites from the Paleoindian period in far northern New Hampshire. Yvonne looked carefully at each of the flakes and shook her head. "These look just like what we're finding up north," she said, the first indication that we might be dealing with something really special: one of the sites left by the earliest inhabitants of New Hampshire.

Sites from the Paleoindian period are rare, and, being the oldest and part of the initial human settlement of North America, they have a special significance for archaeologists. As luck would have it, in my twenty-five years of doing archaeology in New England, this would be the first Paleo site I had ever found, and, in fact, the first I had ever worked on. A few days later, I packed up the flakes and headed to Concord to show them to Dick Boisvert, a leading expert on northeastern Paleoindians and the director of a decades-long research project on Paleoindian sites in New Hampshire's North Country. As the state archaeologist, Dick was also responsible for overseeing compliance with the National Historic Preservation Act and would have to approve any archaeological work at the Keene Middle School. I laid the flakes on a small tray, and Dick whipped off his glasses and proceeded to hold each flake close to his eye. A few minutes went by without a word being spoken, but when he was done, he replaced his glasses, and said, "There's almost no chance these aren't Paleoindian." He confirmed Yvonne's assessment that the stone was rhyolite coming from Jefferson and Berlin, New Hampshire, and chert from the Munsungun Lake region of northern Maine, materials that were only known to occur together on Paleoindian sites.

It was exciting to think that we'd discovered a Paleoindian site, but what kind of site was it? If all that had happened some 11,000 or 12,000 years ago was that a few people stopping to rest took the opportunity to sharpen some of their tools, all that would be here was a small cluster of tiny flakes. This would be an interesting find but provide relatively little information, and not nearly enough for the site to be listed on the National Register. But what if this was just the edge of a richer site? The only way to answer this was to do more excavation, to tighten the interval of the shovel test pits around our find spot and see if we could find more, not only flakes but tools, burned bone, or other sorts of artifacts reflecting a wider range of activities.

Once again, I had to return to SAU 29 and ask for funding and authorization to do more archaeology. I explained what we'd found, what we were trying to learn, how we'd do it, and quickly got the go-ahead. As the pace of planning for the new school accelerated, with ground-breaking imminent, the archaeology was still a small concern. But time was still ticking away, it was now early December, and the ground was about to freeze. We returned to the field immediately and placed a grid of test pits at four-meter intervals around our find spot, planning to extend this out in every direction until we were no longer finding artifacts and to excavate larger one-meter square units to investigate the areas around the most productive test pits. If we didn't find much, or found nothing at all, the school project could proceed unhindered.

It turned out to be bad news for the new middle school. Once again, most of our test pits produced nothing but fine sand, but others produced artifacts that seemed to be arranged in two distinct clusters separated by an empty, artifact-free space. And there were more than just flakes. Four stone tools, two scrapers, a graver for incising or perforating, and a spokeshave for woodworking were recovered, all typical of the forms used by Paleoindians. And directly associated with the tools and flakes in each cluster were fragments of burned bone that Tonya Largy would later identify as having come from medium-to-large-sized mammals. Clearly, there was more going on here than a few minutes of tool sharpening. The different tools reflected a variety of activities, and the burned bone indicated food preparation. Both of these together suggested a habitation site. The site also had structure, with the two distinct clusters suggesting different activity areas, and it was also in pristine condition, with all the artifacts coming from a narrow zone of soil between 20 and 40 cm below surface, in a setting that had never been plowed or disturbed, as far as we could tell, by any other human activity in the more than 10,000 years since it was inhabited. We finished our work in the cold, with the light failing and snowflakes coming down, knowing we had found something of great importance. With a few days' effort, the site had gone from a handful of small flakes to a potentially complex, ancient site that was clearly eligible for listing on the National Register of Historic Places.

Figure 7.1. Garrett Evans (kneeling) and Celine Rainville excavating in the snow at the Tenant Swamp Site, December 2009. (Photograph by Robert Goodby.)

I presented our findings at the next meeting of the building committee, emphasizing the site's age, how intact it was, the fact that it was one of only a handful of known Paleoindian sites in New Hampshire and only the second in Cheshire County, and that it was clearly eligible for the National Register. And it was right where the athletic fields were supposed to go. When I finished, there was dead silence in the room. The architects, planners, engineers, financial experts, and school administrators who had been working for years on this project, with everything tied to the school opening in September of 2011, just stared at me. I looked over at Superintendent Bill Gurney and was taken aback to see his head in his hands. After a moment, he lifted his head up, looked around the room, sighed, and did something completely unexpected.

"You know," he said, "I see some potential for our kids in this."

As with so many federal programs, there are lots of misconceptions about how the National Historic Preservation Act works. It does *not* protect archaeological sites from all types of development, but only those projects that use federal funds or require federal permits. It almost never prevents projects from being completed—even when there's a significant site, the project can continue once some steps, known as mitigation, are taken to offset the harm that will be caused by the site's destruction. The mitigation might involve excavation of a portion of the site, a public education component, or the preservation of an equivalent site somewhere else. And the process is not run by heavy-handed powerful bureaucrats but by a handful of dedicated professionals in the state's underfunded and understaffed historic preservation office, who spend as much time trying to get federal agencies to abide by the law as they do private developers. Often, if the federal agency involved chooses to turn its back, there's little the state can do to enforce the law. With the site at the Keene Middle School, the New Hampshire Division of Historical Resources lobbied long and hard to make sure it got the attention it deserved.

The site was assigned a number (27CH187) in the state's inventory of archaeological sites, and I gave it the formal name of the Tenant Swamp Site. A local paper ran a story on the project with the headline "Chips of Stone Delay Middle School Project," making it a public issue. The question now was what to do about it, and this was worked out in a series of meetings and phone calls over the winter of 2009–2010 between the Division of Historical Resources (acting on behalf of the US Army Corps) and the architects and administrators. In a situation like this, the option of choice is avoidance—simply changing the design of the project to avoid the site. This suggestion produced a decidedly heated response from the architects, as their design utilized every available bit of land, so there was no place to move part of the project. Nor was it possible to reduce or eliminate the athletic fields, as that would jeopardize state certification. Even if it was possible to move the fields, the construction plans called for taking that portion of the terrace down more than ten feet below grade and using the sand as fill in other parts of the project, savings hundreds of thousands of dollars on the cost of trucking sand in from somewhere else.

That left only one option for the school project to go forward, and that was mitigation. The mitigation plan was crafted by the Division of Historical Resources, and included the following:

1. Continued shovel testing further back from the edge of the swamp to see if there were additional clusters of Paleoindian artifacts
2. Complete excavation of every Paleoindian artifact cluster identified
3. Testing on additional SAU 29-owned land along the western and eastern edges of Tenant Swamp
4. A public education component ensuring that the taxpayers of SAU 29 (who were funding the archaeological study) and their children would share in what was learned

The following spring, as soon as I was done with my teaching duties at Franklin Pierce, we began fieldwork, working for the next seven weeks, often seven days a week. My crew consisted of long-time professional field archaeologists and students from Franklin Pierce University, who, having taken my archaeological field school, were qualified to work as professional field technicians. Meanwhile, the work on the school buildings to the north of the site was underway, and we would begin each day by parking, donning hardhats and orange vests, walking through the construction zone and into the woods, taking off the hardhats and vests, and setting to work. We began by extending our grid northwards, excavating an additional 129 test pits, and finding two more clusters of Paleoindian artifacts, with the same types of stone and similar tools. We now had four clusters and would get to completely excavate each one, a remarkable opportunity to study the earliest inhabitants of New Hampshire.

To extract as much information as possible from the site, we enlisted the help of five specialists, each of whom would make a major contribution. Geomorphologist Christopher Dorion would study the site's setting to understand how the landform had been shaped by glacial and post-glacial activity, and what the environment had been like when the Paleoindians occupied it. Geologist Stephen

Pollock of the University of Southern Maine, an expert in sourcing stone artifacts from northeastern archaeological sites, would examine the tools and flakes and determine where the stone was coming from. Heather Rockwell, a doctoral candidate at the University of Wyoming, was an expert in the analysis of microscopic wear patterns on stone tools that reflect what kind of material the tool was used on and what sort of action (cutting, scraping, perforating, drilling, etc.) was being used. Instead of assuming what tools were used for by their shape, Heather would provide concrete evidence of just what was taking place on the site. Finally, the calcined bone would be examined by Tonya Largy and by Maine State Archaeologist Dr. Arthur Spiess, an authority on northeastern Paleoindian sites and a zooarchaeologist with a particular expertise in identifying caribou bone.

At each cluster, we began by placing a one-meter square excavation unit right next to the test pit that had produced artifacts. If we found artifacts, we would place more excavation units adjacent to it, and keep expanding the excavation outwards until the artifacts stopped turning up. By doing so, we hoped to not only recover all the artifacts, but find the edges of each cluster. This had the effect

Figure 7.2. Tenant Swamp Site excavations, view northeast. The Keene Middle School construction site is in the far background. (Photograph by Robert Goodby.)

Figure 7.3. Ed Bouras, excavating a 50-cm quadrant in a 1-meter excavation unit, has just exposed an *in situ* Paleoindian scraping tool. (Photograph by Steve Bayly.)

of turning a single square hole into a larger and larger area, so that a visitor toward the end of the excavation process would see a large, irregularly shaped rectangle.

We were also going to use more refined excavation techniques than we had in the first stages of work. Each one-meter square excavation unit would be subdivided into four 50-cm-square quadrants, and each quadrant would be excavated separately, carefully scraping with the sharp edge of a flat-bladed shovel or trowel, using them almost like a wood plane to shave off the thinnest lens of soil. The soil would be carefully placed in a plastic bucket to be screened through fine, ⅛-inch-mesh screen. This shaving would continue until we had gone down 5 cm from our starting point. All the soil from each 5-cm level in each 50-cm quadrant would be screened at once, and any artifacts bagged together with all the information on their three-dimensional location recorded on the artifact bag, the field forms, and in the master site inventory.

The goal was not only to recover all the artifacts, but to find as many artifacts as possible *in situ*, that is, in their original location, so that their exact three-dimensional location could be recorded on an excavation plan before they came out of the ground. To record depth, a horizontal plane was established by attaching

Figure 7.4. Yvonne Benney Basque recording depth with a line level and tape measure. (Photograph by Steve Bayly.)

a piece of string with a line level to a nail in an adjacent tree stump, pulling the string taut, and measuring downwards with a metric tape measure. Even if small artifacts were missed during excavation, they would likely be recovered in the screen, and we would know which 50-cm quadrant they had come from and how deep they were within a 5-cm margin of error.

As a fan of British police dramas, I am always struck by the similarities between archaeology and detective work. Both are trying to see what people did in the past, and both use material evidence and analysis of where that evidence is found. Both make maps and use photographs to record their evidence. Just like a homicide detective who arrives on the scene of the crime and secures it so the

Figure 7.5. Cory Atkinson (foreground) and Celine Rainville excavating around tree roots at House #2. (Photograph by Robert Goodby.)

evidence can be documented, the ultimate goal of our fieldwork was to produce highly accurate maps of each artifact cluster so we could see their shape, their contents, and any other clues they might reveal about what had taken place here. We didn't know what these maps would show, but as it turns out, these detailed maps would be the most important thing to come out of this site.

In most respects, this was an ideal site for excavation. The artifacts were not deeply buried, the site was remarkably undisturbed, and the soil was fine, dry sand that fell through the screen with only a few shakes. There was only one difficulty: following Murphy's Law, each of our artifact clusters had at least one enormous white pine tree growing in it, and the artifacts we were interested in were among and underneath the roots of these trees. We had to get the artifacts out, recording their location as precisely as possible, but if we undermined the root systems of these venerable trees, and they fell over, they'd not only endanger the archaeologists but dramatically disturb the site, displacing all the artifacts and making our maps worthless. I called Dick Boisvert, asking for advice and expecting sympathy for my predicament. Instead, what I got was a terse "Cut 'em down." We vacated

Figure 7.6. Geomorphologist Chris Dorion in construction trench adjacent to the Tenant Swamp Site. (Photograph by Robert Goodby.)

the site for a day, while skilled lumberjack Ben Northcott carefully took the trees down so their roots didn't move, and they fell away from the excavations. The next day, work resumed.

Early on in our fieldwork, geomorphologist Chris Dorion spent three days on site, examining the soils in our excavation and the deep trenches dug for the school foundation, carefully studying the topography both of the site and general vicinity. He took core samples from Tenant Swamp, collecting deeply buried organic materials that could be radiocarbon dated to establish when the swamp was first formed, and reviewed the existing literature on the glacial and post-glacial geology of the Keene area. This highly scientific work set the scene for the story of the Paleoindians and helped place them in the middle of a remarkable, turbulent period in the natural history of the North American continent.

The story Chris told began with the last episode of glaciation, when, 18,000 years before present, the climate was dramatically colder and the Laurentian ice sheet covered all of New England, with its melting southern edge depositing the sand and rock that would later be called Long Island. At this point, a sheet of ice perhaps a mile thick covered all of New Hampshire, and there was no significant plant or animal life. Shortly after this, a slight shift in the earth's axis started a period of global warming and glacial retreat, with the leading edge of the glacier melting faster than it was advancing, and by 15,000 years ago, most of New Hampshire was ice-free. Left behind were enormous lakes of cold, pure glacial meltwater, including Glacial Lake Ashuelot, which covered the entire Keene area. The slow-moving waters from the melting glacier deposited over two hundred feet of fine sand over the southern part of Keene, creating a delta in the lake that took the form of a braided outwash plain, a level, sandy surface crosscut by shallow, meandering streams of meltwater.

Glacial Lake Ashuelot covered the area for perhaps 400 years, but its waters then began to drain out, downcutting through the fine sediments and carving out the first incarnation of the Ashuelot River valley some 1,000 to 2,000 years before the arrival of the Paleoindians. The climate continued to warm, until 12,900 years ago when brutally cold, windy, unstable weather set in, a climate reversal known as the Younger Dryas that would last for the next 1,300 years. The strong winds of the Younger Dryas picked up the finer sediments of the delta, depositing them in a layer of wind-blown sand known as an aeolian mantle. Chris identified an aeolian mantle at the Tenant Swamp Site, directly below the thin layer of topsoil and above the coarser sands of the outwash plain, and it was from this layer that all the Paleoindian artifacts emerged. We now knew something about when the

Figure 7.7. Active braided outwash plain in Greenland. A comparable process created the deep, level sandy terrace at the Tenant Swamp Site. (Courtesy of Dr. Karl Kreutz, University of Maine.)

site was occupied and could begin to envision the challenges of life in a time of rapid climate change.

Chris had one other surprise in store for us. His soil cores and examination of the topography and the incised, steep edge of the terrace showed that the early Ashuelot River had run right next to the site during Paleoindian times, cutting away at the terrace and only later meandering well to the east. It was the river, not just a wetland, that the Paleoindians encountered, a river whose valley provided an expansive view of the terrain to the south.

This was not a treeless tundra, but a landscape that has no counterpart on earth today, close to active glaciers but too far south and getting too much sunlight for permafrost. Studies of fossilized pollens across New England have shown that the vegetation of the Younger Dryas was markedly different from modern times, likely dominated by patches of conifers, including pine, hemlock, and spruce interspersed with areas of open grassland or meadow. Mount Monadnock, the dominant feature for which the region is named, would have been visible to the east. This was a short-lived, transitional environment, and along with the vegetation different sorts of animals were present. Elsewhere in North America, the distinctive fluted spearpoints of the Paleoindians have been found embedded in the bones of extinct Pleistocene megafauna like mammoths, mastodons, or *Bison antiquus*, a giant version of the modern buffalo, but these animals were rapidly dying off as the first people arrived in New England. Woodland caribou, on the other hand, were thriving and quickly became a staple of the Paleoindian diet.

The four clusters of artifacts were numbered 1 through 4, in the order of their discovery, and excavation began at 1 and 2, which were directly adjacent to each other. As excavation progressed, dozens of stone tools and fragments of burned bone and hundreds of flakes were recovered. As artifact locations were plotted on field maps what had looked like formless scatters of artifacts turned into crisply defined ovals between 12-and-16-feet long and 10-and-12-feet wide. They not only had a defined shape, but there were patterns within them as well. Most obviously, burned bone fragments were recovered from three of the four clusters, and in each, the bone was tightly concentrated in a 2–3-foot area in the center of the oval.

Contrasting with these patterns was something odd in Locus 1 that would turn out to be one of our most important finds. It was a linear arrangement of small pieces of local granitic stone, ranging in size from a golf ball to a baseball, found three feet beyond and running parallel to the edge of the artifact cluster. They looked like natural, unmodified stones, with no evidence of any sort of use,

Figure 7.8. Linear alignment of stones (left) with associated scraper of Munsungun chert (right). (Photograph by Robert Goodby.)

or any indications they had been in a fire. And they were the only stones of this sort that we'd encountered in the pure sand of the high terrace. Fortunately, they came to light while Chris Dorion was on the site, and he confirmed that they were not part of the natural sandy deposits but had been brought to the site from somewhere else, possibly from a nearby rocky streambed. Once the stones were mapped and photographed, they were carefully removed, and a beautifully made scraping tool of Munsungun chert emerged from among them, clearly connecting the stones to the Paleoindian occupation. But why were they there?

The answer to this riddle would come from the clusters themselves. Similar circular or oval clusters had been documented at a handful of other northeastern Paleoindian sites, and some of these were interpreted as the location of houses, likely hide-covered tents. When the occupants moved and the tents were taken down, what remained was an oval or circular cluster of debris reflecting where the tent had been. The idea that these were house floors was powerfully shaped by what cultural anthropologists had learned about the indigenous cultures of northern Canada, like the Naskapi or Inuit, who hunted caribou in a cold subarctic environment. A description of a Naskapi house published in 1907 provides a powerful analog for understanding the artifact clusters at Tenant Swamp:

> The dwellings, for both winter and summer, are tents or tipis of reindeer skins sewed together, and measuring 10 to 18 ft. at the base and 10 to 14 ft. high. The floor is carpeted with young spruce branches, except around the central fire-place; the smoke escapes through an opening in the top of the tipi where the supporting poles are brought together . . . The outer edge of the interior is slightly raised above the center of the floor, affording a slope for the occupants when sleeping . . .

Immediately around the heat and light of the fire was a work area, where people sheltering from the cold could prepare food, make stone tools or clothing, or any other work best done indoors. This matched the Tenant Swamp clusters, where the burned bone, marking the location of a fire, was dead-center in the middle of an artifact-strewn work area.

But what about the sleeping area? Logically, this would be mostly artifact-free, as people would not want to sleep on or near the sharp-edged flakes,

Figure 7.9. Inuit family by hide-covered oval tent in northern Quebec, early twentieth century. (Courtesy of the National Museums of Canada.)

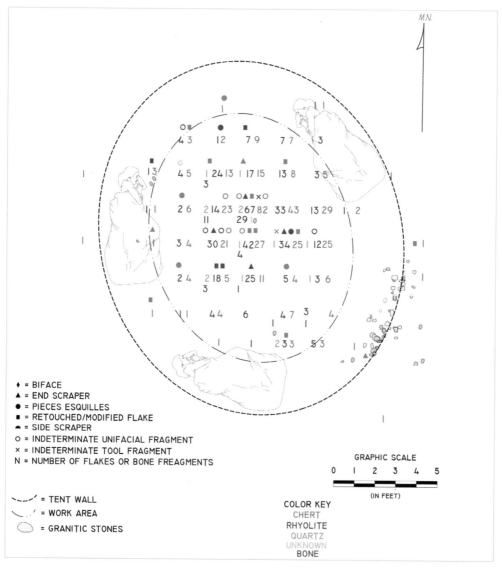

Figure 7.10. Map of House #1. (Map produced by Garrett Evans.)

and this is where the odd linear stone alignment came into play. Even without knowing the function of these stones, their alignment, exactly parallel to the edge of the work area, suggested they had been pushed up against the wall of the tent, and thus marked its location. I asked Garrett Evans, who was producing the final versions of the site maps, to extend the line formed by the stones around the entire work area. Once this was done, I asked him to create scaled illustrations of sleeping people and see if they would fit in the space between the work area and the wall of the tent. He did, and they fit perfectly.

Suddenly, everything had fallen into place. With these maps we could walk into four houses from the end of the Pleistocene and see where single families cooked, worked, and slept, and begin to ask nosy questions about what they had done and how they differed from their neighbors, if at all. We could learn what they ate, what sort of work they were doing, and how their domestic space was organized. This was time-travel on a grand scale, and the clarity and detail of each map provided one of the best examples of Paleoindian house floors in eastern North America.

To the relief of the SAU 29 building committee, we completed our field-work on Friday, June 26. I sent an email to Dick Boisvert that evening, telling him we were done; he sent an email to the US Army Corps of Engineers, and on Monday heavy machinery moved on to the formerly quiet, shaded terrace, taking down trees and removing ten feet of sand. Was there anything we had missed? It was likely. Our shovel-testing interval was eight meters, about twenty-six feet, and every one of our house floors could have fallen within that interval. What we likely had was a sample of what was there, and we would have to live with that. It's the nature of any sampling strategy that not everything can be looked at, that some things will be missed, but that, with a little luck, what you have will reflect that whole you aren't able to completely see. And having four thoroughly docu-mented Paleoindian house floors is no small thing. But I've thought about those missed house floors ever since.

It's almost always the case when you're working on a complex, interesting site that the most important discoveries are made after the excavation is completed, when the data is analyzed, and new information comes to light. As soon as we were done with fieldwork, the burned bone was sent to Tonya Largy. Most of the fragments were small and non-descript and could only be identified as mammals, but Tonya was able to identify one fragment from House #3 as part of an otter pelvis. The otter has seldom been recovered from Paleoindian sites but would have been valued for its meat and waterproof pelt. Finding the remains of an otter at Tenant Swamp also made sense once we knew the site had been on the edge of the Ashuelot River. Art Spiess identified a bone fragment from House #1 as a caribou metacarpal or metatarsal, and a fragment from House #2 as a caribou proximal phalange. Interestingly, both are foot bones, and both were from imma-ture animals, likely a yearling in the case of the phalange. Other bones from the site resembled cervid, the class that includes deer and caribou, but were too frag-mentary to make a precise identification. Not surprisingly, the people at Tenant Swamp were caribou hunters.

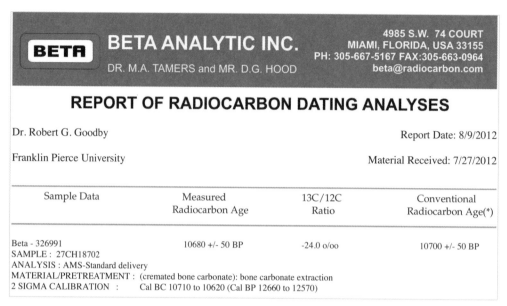

Figure 7.11. Radiocarbon dating report on burned bone from House #2

One of the challenges in studying New England Paleoindian sites has been obtaining reliable radiocarbon dates. For reasons that aren't well understood, the Paleoindian people did not, like their descendants, leave behind well-defined rock-lined hearths chock full of burned wood fragments, and Tenant Swamp was no exception. The tight clusters of burned bone fragments in the center of the tents did not have any associated wood charcoal. Fortunately, recent advances in radiocarbon dating had made it possible to date minute quantities of burned bone, and after Tonya and Art had completed their analysis, a sample of bone from the middle of House #2 was sent off to Beta Analytic, Inc. for accelerator mass spectrometry (AMS) radiocarbon dating. A few weeks later the results arrived, and they were startling: the bone dated between 12,570 and 12,660 years before present. There is no older dated Paleoindian site in New England, and, as close as we could get given the limits of the dating technology, we were looking at the very first people to live in the Monadnock region, the very beginning of the human story, and the answer to that question my students didn't know: when the first human beings arrived in New England.

Hunkering Down: Winter in the Younger Dryas

Tenant Swamp was not the first place where Paleoindian house floors have been identified in eastern North America. At a number of other sites, artifact clusters representing house floors are accompanied by other clusters outside the houses. These clusters, where one or two types of specialized tools predominate, were where particular activities took place, such as tool-making, butchering, or hide-working. But at Tenant Swamp, as far as we could tell, there was an unusually wide array of activities taking place indoors, and no evidence of anything happening outside.

Why? The most obvious explanation is that this was a wintertime occupation, and winters in the Younger Dryas were not to be trifled with. Geologists have found ancient dune features where windborne sands were sculpted by heavy winds from the northwest. The combination of bitterly cold temperatures and howling winds, along with winter snow, would have made the outdoors a difficult and dangerous place. Like all hunter-gatherers in northern latitudes, the Paleoindian people would have put up a reserve of food, dried or cached where it would stay frozen, to get them through the worst months of the winter. And they would, for the most part, have stayed put, spending far more time in a small, enclosed space than anyone cared to, making preparations for a spring that couldn't come soon enough. Those preparations would leave their own traces in over two hundred stone tools distributed among the four houses.

As excavation was coming to an end, Heather Rockwell began her work looking for microscopic evidence of use-wear on these tools that would reveal exactly what they had been used for. As this was a Paleoindian site, we expected to find fluted spear points. Instead, we were finding a variety of tools used to make other tools or to work leather. One of the most common were scrapers, flaked on a single side to create a steep edge. Archaeologists have long assumed that these were used primarily for hide-scraping, removing the tissue from the inside of an animal hide as a step toward turning it into clothing, containers, or the covering for a tent. Heather's analysis confirmed this, finding two kinds of wear on these tools: hide scraping, and evidence of hafting, created when the scraper was set in a bone or wooden handle.

Figure 7.12. End scrapers from House #1. Artifacts 40-1, 294-1, 310-1, and 371-1 are made of Mount Jasper rhyolite, and 216-1, 598-1, and 361-1/369-1 are made of Munsungun chert. (Photograph by Steve Bayly.)

One of the other things archaeologists have long assumed, something Heather's analysis could not shed light on, was that hide scraping was women's work, and that the presence of these tools reflected the presence of women. As dozens of these tools came to light in the first weeks of excavation, without any evidence of the fluted points assumed to reflect male hunting, we began to wonder about what sort of site this was and made jokes about having discovered the earliest feminist collective.

Other tools shed light on other activities taking place in these tents. Spokeshaves, made with a concave bit for shaping wooden handles or shafts, had wear from wood scraping and cutting. Broken, battered fragments of tools used as miniature wedges for splitting bone, antler, or wood, known to archaeologists as *pieces esquilles*, a term originating from the study of the French Upper Paleolithic, also indicated toolmaking. A large chopping tool fashioned of coarse-grained local stone and broken into pieces was found on the floor of House #3. Also recovered were intricately shaped gravers with stylus-like tips whose function has puzzled

600.1

1 CM

Figure 7.13. Chopping tool from House #3. (Photograph by Steve Bayly.)

archaeologists, who have suggested they were used for everything from perforating leather to fine engraving on bone or antler and even for tattooing. Whatever their use was, it was so delicate it left no traces Heather could detect.

The most numerous tools were utilized flakes, possibly picked up from the debris left behind by flintknapping, whose naturally sharp edges could be used as expedient tools for all sorts of uses. Over and over, on the utilized flakes Heather detected evidence of cutting and, occasionally, wear from hide-scraping. But on three of these tools, she found something unexpected: evidence of prehension, the

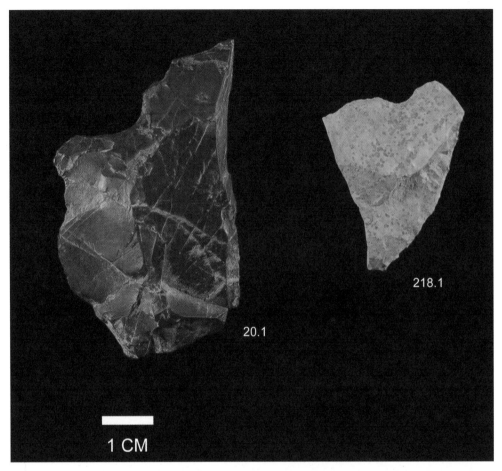

Figure 7.14. Spokeshaves from House #2. The one on the left, made of Munsungun chert, had evidence of prehension. The one on the right is made of Mount Jasper rhyolite. (Photograph by Steve Bayly.)

technical term for being gripped in the human hand. Some of these cutting tools had been held so tightly and used so intensively, that almost 13,000 years later Heather could see the distinctive polish that this person's hand left behind. One of the spokeshaves and a hide-scraping tool from House #1 also had evidence for prehension.

As I read her report, I was taken back to that afternoon in the summer of 1984 when I became an archaeologist, feeling that odd, intimate sense of connection to a stranger from another culture and time. After all the science, all the focus on material things, we are ultimately interested in real, flesh-and-blood people who had individual personalities, names, and identities, even if the tools of archaeology leave us poorly equipped to see them. With these cutting tools,

Figure 7.15. Utilized flake cutting tools. Numbers 734 and 762 have evidence of prehension. (Photograph by Steve Bayly.)

though, I was holding the same objects they held, I knew something about what they'd done, where they did it, and I could see where their hands had been, leaving the exact traces that my hand would leave if I were doing the same thing. I could imagine myself in their place and feel empathy, that most powerful and uniquely human trait. Having travelled from objects to an actual person, though, I was still left looking into a void, wondering what they had been cutting with such determination. Was it a new tent covering? A pair of warm winter boots crafted from otter pelts and caribou hide? Or an ornate jacket for a young woman's coming-of-age ceremony planned for the spring? Once again, archaeology can lead you to those questions, ones that can't be answered but are worth asking anyway and that can be the basis for stories that fit within the framework provided by the broken bits of tools and by what anthropology tells us about human behavior in general.

Almost a month into our excavation, we had yet to find any evidence of hunting. At other Paleoindian sites, hunting is reflected by fluted points, the fragments of points broken in hunting, and by the distinctive channel flakes produced when the "flute" is created by removing a long, shallow flake down the length of the blade. Finally, a tiny tool fragment from House #3 was identified as the corner,

Figure 7.16. Gravers from House #4. (Photograph by Steve Bayly.)

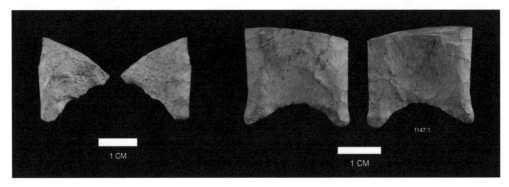

Figure 7.17. Obverse and reverse view of the fluted-point ear from House #3 (left) and the fluted-point base from House #2. (Photograph by Steve Bayly.)

or ear, of a fluted point that had been badly damaged by being used as a wedge at the end of its life. But that was it, until the very end of the excavation, when the base of a fluted point was found at the southern end of House #2, immediately outside the tent wall. And that really was it: of more than two hundred stone tools, only these two broken fragments had any connection to hunting. This was surprising, but perhaps it shouldn't have been. The lack of evidence for hunting fit with this being a winter occupation, when people were eating stored meat cached in the fall and not venturing into the brutal cold and snow in search of game.

How were these four houses related to each other? They were similar in shape, and the differences in size (House #2 being approximately 25% larger than House #3 and House #4) could easily be explained by having a slightly larger family group. There were no obvious differences in the number or variety of tools among the houses, as each family seemed to have the same tool kit, used for the same sorts of activities. This is exactly what anthropologists would expect of any

	House 1	House 2	House 3	House 4	Totals
Size (in Feet)	**16x14**	**20x15**	**15x12**	**15x12**	
Bifacial Tools (Various Functions)	0	6	4	5	15
Chopper	0	0	1	0	1
End Scrapers	7	5	4	4	20
Side Scrapers	0	1	2	6	9
Gravers	0	7	4	7	18
Pieces Esquilles	6	3	1	5	15
Retouched Flakes/Cutting Tools	14	26	32	22	94
Spokeshaves	0	2	2	2	6
Fluted Points	0	1	1	0	2
Unifacial Tools (Various Functions)	8	6	7	6	27
Tool Fragments	2	2	5	0	9
Totals	**37**	**59**	**63**	**57**	**216**

Figure 7.18. Comparison of house size and tool kits

small-scale society, where there would not be significant status differences, social inequality, or an elaborate division of labor. While different individuals undoubtedly had varying levels of skill when it came to hide working, flintknapping, or healing, it would make no sense to have only one person or one family have exclusive mastery of something everyone needed for survival.

While the four houses were similar, were they occupied at the same time? Were these four related families living together during a single winter, or a single family that had returned to this place during four different winters? And how could this possibly be determined? At the Vail Paleoindian Site in western Maine, archaeologists were able to conclusively establish that separate house floors were contemporaneous when they found broken fragments from a single fluted point in separate houses. This was interpreted as evidence of sharing, so that a freshly killed caribou would be divided among the various families, and one house would wind up with the part of the carcass containing a broken tip of a fluted point. Meanwhile, the hunter whose point had broken would remove the base from their spear shaft, dropping it in a second house. When archaeologists fit the two

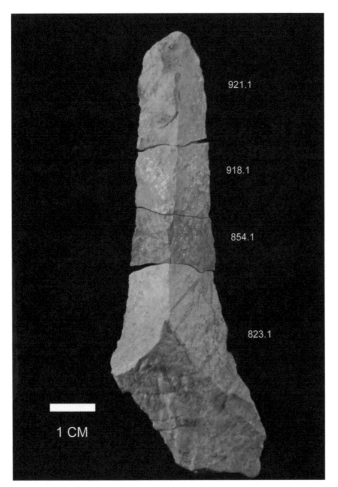

921.1

918.1

854.1

823.1

1 CM

Figure 7.19. Four conjoining fragments of a broken cutting tool made of Mount Jasper rhyolite from House #3. (Photograph by Steve Bayly.)

fragments together, it was clear that the houses were occupied at exactly the same time by families who worked together and shared their resources.

Showing this type of relationship at Tenant Swamp would be much harder, as there were almost no spear points. Many of the other tools were broken, and many fragments could be refit, but only within single houses. Two separate systematic efforts, the first by Ed Bouras and the second by Gail Golec and me, were made to find matching tool fragments that would connect two or more of the houses at Tenant Swamp, and both were unsuccessful. The strong similarity of the artifacts from these houses suggest they were not far apart in time, but whether they were from a single winter or from a number of different winter encampments stretched over a few centuries remains unanswered. The relative locations of each house didn't shed any light on this question. House #2 is directly adjacent to House #1, a mere ten feet to the north, suggesting (but not proving) they were

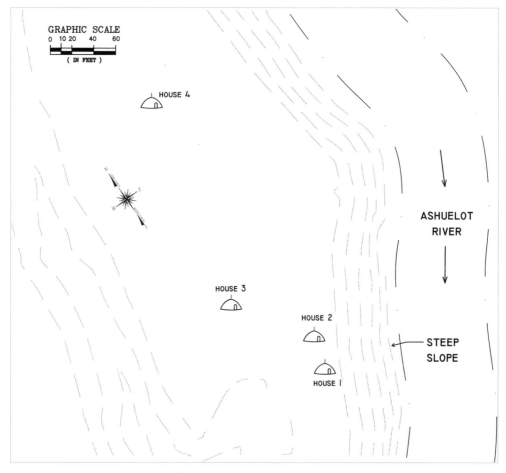

Figure 7.20. Locations of the four houses at the Tenant Swamp Site. (Map produced by Garrett Evans.)

contemporaneous. House #3 is 60 feet northwest of House #2, and House #4 is 130 feet north of House #3, within shouting distance, but clearly at some remove.

The Tenant Swamp houses also made me question how archaeologists have read gender from stone tools. It didn't make sense that, if little or nothing was going on outdoors, that women were doing most or all the work in these houses, while the other half of the population was sitting idly. Wood, leather, bone, antler, and stone . . . these materials were basic to the survival of everyone, and it is far more likely that these activities were communal. Not only would adults have been making tools, but they would have been instructing their children and grand-children, with the winter being the perfect time for lessons, not only on how to fashion a tool from stone, but how to use the phases of the moon to predict the movements of caribou, what sort of plants were useful treatments for common ailments like headaches, and how the Creator had shaped their world at the beginning of time. The work of education was also happening in these tents, which was as important for their survival as any of the activities that left more obvious traces.

The Paleoindian Social Universe

It has long been a common misconception that hunting and gathering people have simple lives, lacking in developed culture and consumed by the daily struggle of trying to survive with only the most primitive of tools. When cultural anthropologists in the 1960s began studying the handful of hunter-gatherer societies still left in the world, they found something very different: they were societies with far more leisure time than people in agricultural or industrial societies, with complex languages, rich artistic traditions, and complex cosmologies that accounted for their origins and the age-old questions of human mortality. Their social relationships were equally complex, as they lived in a world where almost everyone was defined as kin, and elaborate rules governed patterns of marriage and residence. This would have almost certainly been the case for the Paleoindian people at Tenant Swamp.

Once Heather Rockwell had completed her analysis, the stone artifacts were delivered to Dr. Stephen Pollock at the University of Southern Maine. Steve looked at the type of stone, its grain size, internal structure, color, and the presence of tiny fossils. He compared these to the characteristics of stone from known quarry sources in northeastern North America and was able to confirm what Yvonne Benney Basque and Dick Boisvert had said—that almost all the stone at Tenant Swamp came from three far-distant sources in northern New England. The closest of these was in Jefferson, New Hampshire, approximately 110 miles north of Tenant Swamp, and on the other side of the White Mountains. Only a handful of the Tenant Swamp tools had come from Jefferson. Half of the tools had originated from the small quarry at the top of Mount Jasper outside the city of Berlin, 120 miles from Tenant Swamp and north of Mount Washington, the highest peak of the White Mountains. Almost all the remaining tools came from sources around Munsungun Lake in north-central Maine, some 350 miles northeast of Tenant Swamp.

How had this stone moved? In earlier times, anthropologists imagined bands of hunters following migrating herds of caribou, travelling hundreds of miles in a year, which could have them in northern Maine in the summer and wintering on the edge of Tenant Swamp. The only problem with that scenario is that migrating caribou can easily travel twenty miles or more a day, far faster than humans on foot with infants, children, and elderly people, and that it's only the barren-ground caribou that migrate long distances—the woodland caribou that were most likely hunted by the Tenant Swamp people do not travel great distances from one season to the next. Even if it wasn't in pursuit of caribou and travel was done by canoe, it would have taken people the better part of two months to make such a journey—and Munsungun was not the only place stone was coming from.

Rather than long-distance travel, it was the social world that explains why this exotic stone was at Tenant Swamp. A typical hunter-gatherer band might have between thirty and eighty people, living in small, related family groups. One of the common rules of these bands was exogamy: when it was time to marry, your mate had to come from outside your band. Either the husband or wife would leave their natal band to live with their spouse's band. As a result, bands were not isolated but had strong ties to other bands with whom they interacted on a regular basis. These bands were where your brothers, sisters, cousins, aunts, uncles, and grandparents could be found, and a highlight of any year's travels would be reuniting with these close family members at some location prearranged by tradition or plans made the previous year. Just as you share many, but not all, of your cousin's relatives, each of these bands would be related in turn to other bands, creating extensive kin networks that stretched across much of the northeast.

There were many advantages to living in this network of related family bands. One was what the cultural anthropologists call "fluid band membership," meaning that an individual or family always had the option of going to live with another band, knowing their family would take them in. This helped if a band grew too large or if disagreements with family members (another human universal) made it attractive to go live somewhere else. Another advantage of these networks was that families would share information, so knowledge of the natural and social environment could extend for hundreds of miles and draw on the experience of thousands of people. This information would be shared when the bands got together, important occasions that would have been discussed with anticipation during the long winters in the tents on the edge of the river.

Family and kinship are human universals: all people make a distinction between those who are kin and those who aren't. And whenever family members come together after a long absence, there are other universals, including feasting, talking, sharing, and gift-giving. If you have access to some rare commodity, that will probably be what you bring, much as I once took a quart of New Hampshire

Figure 7.21. Keene Middle School under construction on the last day of archaeological fieldwork, July 2010. (Photograph by Robert Goodby.)

maple syrup to friends in New Mexico (stowing it, most unwisely, in my checked bag on the airplane). For Paleoindians living close to a good source of stone, that's what would be taken to the family gathering and shared with relatives, who in turn would share it with others they were related to. The exotic stone at Tenant Swamp doesn't reflect long-distance travel by isolated bands of stone-age people, but extensive, rich, and complex family networks that moved material, information, and culture over a vast area, seen in the appearance of Jefferson rhyolite at Paleoindian sites in southern Massachusetts and Munsungun chert at sites as far south as New Jersey. It was indeed a large world that these people inhabited.

The new Keene Middle School opened on time, admitting its first students in September of 2011. It is a superb facility, with modern, well-lit classrooms; a large, state-of-the-art auditorium; and, in the back of the school, modern athletic fields on the edge of Tenant Swamp where the Paleoindian site had been. That fall, I was invited to give a presentation to the entire school on the people who had once lived on their campus, and I have returned every fall since to speak to the incoming sixth-grade class. In the meantime, the teachers at the Middle

Figure 7.22. The new Keene Middle School. (Photograph by Miranda Nelken. Courtesy of Keene Middle School.)

School began to fulfill Bill Gurney's vision, incorporating information from the site into their social studies and science courses, and raising money to produce accurate replicas of the stone tools and to build a boardwalk into Tenant Swamp that featured interpretive signage on the Paleoindian camp. In a society polarized over the proper role of government regulation, this was an example of how such regulations work best, balancing competing interests to produce a beneficial outcome. The region got a wonderful school, priceless information on the region's history was saved, and, for decades to come, every Keene Middle School student will learn when the first human beings arrived in New England.

Figure 7.23. Bob Goodby demonstrating the use of an atlatl, or spear thrower, at the Keene Middle School, standing just to the west of where House #3 was located. (Photograph by Steve Hooper. Courtesy of the *Keene Sentinel*.)

Figure 7.24. Interpretive signage, Tenant Swamp boardwalk. (Photograph by Gail Golec.)

Coda

The Tenant Swamp site produced wonderful scientific data about the first people to see Mount Monadnock. But it can also give us a basis for empathy and imagination to help break down the barriers we set up between science and the humanities, between objective knowledge of material things and the created, imagined, intuited world of real people. Despite all the differences of time and culture, the Paleoindians were human beings, exactly as we are human beings, and we can use archaeological data to enter their world, to travel back in time and imagine the smells of a low-burning fire and animal skins, the snapping and rumpling sound made by the walls of a hide-covered tent buffeted by a deadly cold wind, and the close, musty feel of a small space lived in for months. We can hear sharp clicks as stone strikes stone, and the sound of the old stories, told yet again to children who have long since become inattentive. We can imagine a grandmother's cough, worse now than at the beginning of the winter, and the sharp cry of a newborn who feels the blast of icy air every time a tent flap is lifted, revealing a glimpse of a mountain to the east, standing alone in a snow-covered landscape.

Figure 7.25. Mount Monadnock, view east from Keene, New Hampshire. (Courtesy of Steve Hooper.)

CHAPTER 8
Survival, Resistance, Renaissance

Almost thirty years ago, I sat nervously in the office of Nanepashemet (Anthony Pollard), director of the Wampanoag Indian Program at Plimoth Plantation. Immersed in my doctoral dissertation on the elaborate Native ceramics of the seventeenth century, I had come to ask him to share his people's history on the place of pottery in Wampanoag culture, and, with luck, to get some hints about what the elaborate decorations meant. He tilted his head back and looked at me with skepticism. "It's become really trendy for you archaeologists to talk to Indians," he said.

I was taken aback. "Yes," I replied, "it has." And we sat in silence for a while, until Nani sighed, smiled, and began talking. Our conversation lasted well over an hour. I asked him who made ceramic pots, what they were used for, why they were decorated, what the decorations meant, and what the nature of tribal differences was. It was a wonderful discussion, in which he generously shared much of what he could, but as our meeting drew to a close, he looked down at his hands and spoke with a note of sadness in his voice: "These sorts of questions are hard for Native people," he said. "We feel like we should know all the answers . . . but so much has been lost."

As the archaeological sites of the Monadnock region show, its history does not begin in 1620, or even 1492, but almost 13,000 years before the *Mayflower* made first landfall on the scrub-oak-covered dunes of the Wampanoag homeland. Even the first contact with Europeans, shrouded in scanty historic records, likely dates to the very late-fifteenth or early sixteenth century, years before the *Mayflower*. The first recorded contact between Europeans and Native people in New England occurred in 1524, when the explorer Giovanni de Verrazano described the people of Narragansett Bay, Algonquian-speaking cousins of the Abenaki, saying:

They exceed us in size, and they are of a very fair complexion, some incline more to a white and others to a tawny color; their faces are sharp, and their hair long and black, upon the adorning of which they bestow great pains; their eyes are black and sharp, their expressions mild and pleasant . . . they are the most beautiful and have the most civil customs that we found on this voyage.

It is almost certain, given the Native people's extensive, long-standing social networks, that the news of these strange, hairy, pock-marked, malodorous beings moved quickly across the northeast (sixteenth-century Europeans, unlike Native people, viewed bathing as unhealthy and tended to do it only seasonally). Trade began shortly after these initial contacts, and if Native people from the Monadnock region didn't see Europeans while visiting their kin along the coast, they would soon see the growing number of European goods circulating among Native people. A trade in beaver pelts and other commodities produced by Native people developed, along with a new currency of shell beads, known as wampum and produced by Native people in southern New England using drills made of European iron. Wampum facilitated exchange between the various Native communities and the English, French, and Dutch flocking to northeastern North America. European cloth, iron tools, brass and copper kettles, beads and other ornaments, firearms, and alcohol were increasingly incorporated into Native cultures.

Talking to Indians in New England was, in fact, something new. For years, most archaeologists had accepted the widespread notion that the Native cultures of New England were gone, their carriers driven to the edge of extinction by the epidemics and violence of the seventeenth and eighteenth centuries. The few survivors, it was believed, fled to Canada or hid on the margins of White society, rapidly losing their traditional language and lifestyle as they intermarried and assimilated. In New Hampshire, the epidemic of 1616–1617 likely took a huge toll, wiping out as much as 95% of the population. Following this, the carnage of King Philip's War (1675–1676), the first widespread, coordinated effort by the native inhabitants to drive the English invaders out, spread into the southern part of the state. In the eighteenth century, the French and Indian Wars turned southern New Hampshire into a dangerous frontier. The Abenaki, backed by their French allies in Quebec, raided the English settlements encroaching on their homeland and were attacked in turn by English colonists and their Mohawk allies. The violence was exacerbated by bounties paid for Indian scalps by the colonial governments, who offered substantial sums (often fifty pounds or more) for the scalp of a man, with lesser amounts for the scalps of women and children. The scalp bounty also provided an incentive for White incursions and eventual settlement in Abenaki lands.

Only a few rare archaeological sites give us insight into this period, the most notable being the Fort Hill Site in Hinsdale. Occupied for less than a year, from the fall of 1663 to May of 1664, this village, unlike any known site from the pre-Contact period, had been set in a defensible location, on a flat-topped,

1 CM

Figure 8.1. Partially reconstructed Contact-period ceramic pot, AD 1663–1664, Fort Hill Site, Hinsdale, New Hampshire. (Courtesy of Matthew Boulanger.) Typical of pots from this period, it has a high, peaked castellation, an elaborately decorated collar, and a constricted neck. The projecting decoration immediately below the peak of the castellation, once thought to be an ear of corn, is found on ceramic vessels across much of New England in the seventeenth century.

steep-sided hill set back from the Connecticut River. Excavations by Peter Thomas of the University of Massachusetts documented dwelling sites, large storage pits, and an array of artifacts of European manufacture, ranging from glass beads, gunflints, and musket parts to knives, scissors, hatchets, and Jesuit rings obtained from French missionaries. Also recovered were sherds of Native pottery with ornate and complex decorations, one of the few traditional forms of technology that survived in this period of rapid change. Following Thomas's excavation, what remained of the site was largely destroyed by the haphazard digging of metal detector enthusiasts, vandals who left the site a pock-marked ruin with no record of what they found or where it is now housed.

After the American Revolution, the Abenaki seemed to disappear from the Monadnock region, beginning that period of invisibility that made it easy for later historians to deny they had ever really been here. What really happened is, of course, more complicated, and more interesting. After a century or more of travel back and forth to the home of their French allies in Quebec, many Abenaki families settled there, establishing villages at places like Odanak (Saint Francis) that remain Native communities to this day. Others chose to stay, keeping a low profile on the margins of English society, playing down or hiding their Indian identity. Many also kept up a residence pattern with deep traditional roots, moving seasonally between communities in Quebec and their traditional home-lands to the south, always maintaining that same low profile. Anyone looking for Abenaki presence during the nineteenth and early twentieth centuries has to look closely, but once you do, you find evidence almost everywhere.

The Native people in nineteenth-century New Hampshire and Vermont were often misidentified. With their dark hair, dark complexions, and peripatetic movements, they were sometimes called Gypsies, people who would suddenly appear, spend a few weeks or a season camping, fishing, and trapping on the outskirts of town, maybe doing odd jobs for White people from time to time, and then disappearing. Native women would sometimes work as itinerant doctresses and midwives, using traditional Native methods to provide medical care to isolated White communities in a time and place where "modern" medicine was inaccessible.

The arrival of the railroad in the mid-nineteenth century had a transforma-tive effect on Native cultures and their survival. Trains made tourism easy and affordable, bringing large numbers of visitors to the growing resort communi-ties in the mountains and beside the picturesque lakes of New Hampshire and Vermont. As the tourists stepped off the trains, they often encountered peddlers offering finely made ash woodsplint baskets. These peddlers were Native people, often Abenaki, who survived by adapting a traditional art form to the tastes of White tourists. Many of these Native people still hid their true identity, so that a history of Lebanon, New Hampshire, describing a 1920s destination called the Esculapian Springs, could note that "Gypsies camped next to the river selling their baskets to old U.S. Route 4 travelers." As time went on, these baskets were increasingly identified as Indian baskets for White customers who no longer saw Indians as a threat but as a rustic novelty. With a steady demand, this art form flourished, and today Abenaki basket makers are recognized as fine artists whose work is funded by state arts councils, exhibited in museums, and fetches considerable sums in art galleries and auctions.

One of the remarkable stories of Abenaki survival in the Monadnock region is that of the Sadoques family. In the 1880s, Israel Sadoques and his wife Mary (Watso) Sadoques left Odanak and travelled down the Connecticut River by canoe, looking for a place to live. They eventually settled in Keene, New Hampshire, raised a large family and became prominent, popular members of the community, where they became known as "Keene's Indians." Israel made a living making and selling baskets and tanning hides and became a deacon of a local church; one of his daughters opened a millinery shop on the square in downtown Keene. It would seem a sign of considerable progress that an Abenaki family could live openly and with such acceptance at the turn of the twentieth century, but even here the specter of invisibility intruded. A recent museum exhibit on the family curated by Sadoques descendant Lynn Keating Murphy included a remarkable document, the birth certificate of Elizabeth Sadoques, the last of the Sadoques children, born in May of 1897. In this certificate the "color" of both her parents is recorded as Indian, but Elizabeth's color is listed as White.

The family story is that, in a tribute to the high esteem the Sadoques family was held in, the staff at the hospital assumed they were doing them a favor by removing Elizabeth's Indian identity.

Being Indian in northern New England became even harder in the first decades of the twentieth century when the new "science" of eugenics swept the western world. First popularized by Francis Galton, a cousin of Charles Darwin, the movement assumed that poverty, sexual immorality, and criminal behavior were the result of inferior genetics, rather than the consequences of unjust social and economic policies. Eugenics sought to remedy these problems through programs of state-sponsored selective breeding. What this meant in practice was

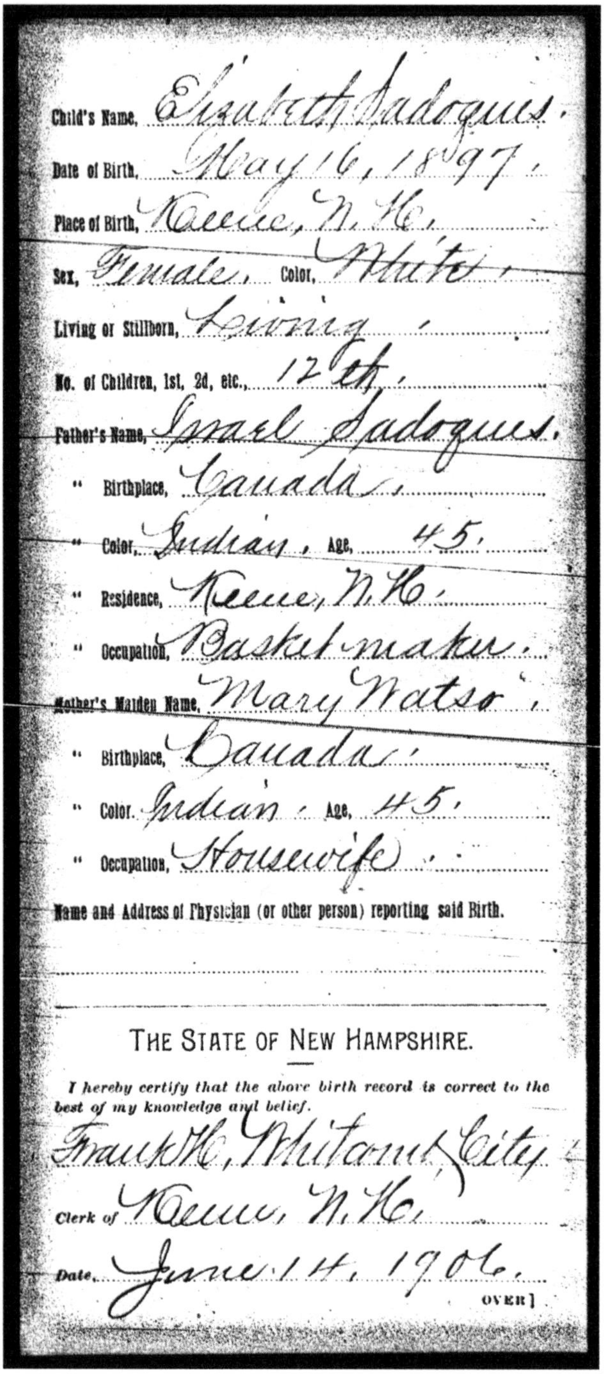

Child's Name, Elizabeth Sadoques.
Date of Birth, May 16, 1897.
Place of Birth, Keene, N. H.
Sex, Female. Color, White.
Living or Stillborn, Living.
No. of Children, 1st, 2d, etc., 12th.
Father's Name, Israel Sadoques.
" Birthplace, Canada.
" Color, Indian. Age, 45.
" Residence, Keene, N. H.
" Occupation, Basket-maker.
Mother's Maiden Name, Mary Watso.
" Birthplace, Canada.
" Color, Indian. Age, 45.
" Occupation, Housewife.
Name and Address of Physician (or other person) reporting said Birth.

THE STATE OF NEW HAMPSHIRE.

I hereby certify that the above birth record is correct to the best of my knowledge and belief.

Frank H. Whitcomb, City
Clerk of Keene, N. H.
Date, June 14, 1906.
OVER]

Figure 8.2. Birth certificate of Elizabeth Sadoques. (*New Hampshire, U.S., Birth Index, 1659–1900* [database on-line]. Provo, UT, USA: Ancestry.com Operations. Inc., 2013.)

Figure 8.3. Elizabeth Sadoques, 1916 high school graduation photo. (Courtesy of Joyce Heywood and the Historical Society of Cheshire County.)

that women from poor and disadvantaged families were sterilized, often without their knowledge and almost always against their will, in state-funded programs.

Vermont was one of a handful of states that embraced eugenics, and under the leadership of University of Vermont scientist Henry Perkins the state targeted particular groups for systematic sterilization. Notable among these were the French Canadians, believed to be an inferior and degenerate race whose French language, Catholicism, and large families threatened the dominance of White, English Protestant culture in Vermont. Another targeted group were "Gypsies," people with dark complexions and dark hair who sold baskets and other crafts and moved from place to place. Sterilizing these "Gypsies" was made easier by a provision in the law that made the children of all parents lacking fixed abodes wards of the state. Perkins knew these were not Romany Gypsies from Europe, but still saw them as a degenerate stock of people who were disproportionately poor and prone to criminal behavior. Most of them were, in fact, Abenaki, and some of today's Abenaki families carry very bitter memories of the forced sterilizations of this period.

A common response to eugenics and other forms of discrimination was for Abenaki parents to not tell their children they were Indian, thinking their lives

119

would be better if they and the hostile White world didn't know. I have worked with many Abenaki people who did not find out they were Native until they were well into adulthood. This self-imposed invisibility, done in the name of survival, is a powerful form of cultural destruction. Most people learn who we are from birth, from our parents, grandparents, and the community that surrounds us. How do you reclaim an identity denied to you in childhood? This is one of the greatest challenges facing many Abenaki people today.

Why did archaeologists in New England just begin to talk to Native people in the 1980s? Native Americans and archaeologists have a long and difficult relationship, much of it centering on the treatment of Native burials. Native people almost universally object to the disturbance of their ancestral burial sites, but archaeologists recognize human remains as a unique source of data about the diet, health, demography, and spiritual lives of past people. Even before landing at Plymouth, the Pilgrims found Native burials while exploring on Cape Cod. In one instance, in an account by William Bradford described in *Mourt's Relations*, they displayed unusual sensitivity:

> We found a little path to certain heaps of sand, one whereof was covered with old mats, and had a wooding thing like a mortar whelmed on the top of it, and an earthen pot laid in a little hole at the end thereof. We, musing what it might be, digged and found a bow, and, as we thought, arrows, but they were rotten. We supposed there were many other things, but because we deemed them graves, we put in the bow again and made it up as it was, and left the rest untouched, *because we thought it would be odious unto them to ransack their sepulchers* [emphasis added].

Later, another burial ground was encountered, but treated somewhat differently:

> We came into the plain ground we found a place like a grave, but it was much bigger and longer than any we had yet seen. It was also covered with boards, so as we mused what it should be, and resolved to dig it up.

To their surprise, they found the recently buried remains of a man with yellow hair, dressed in European sailor's clothes, but buried in a Native fashion, covered with red ocher. Buried with him was a small bundle:

> We opened the less bundle likewise, and found of the same powder in it, and the bones and head of a little child. About the legs and other parts of it was bound strings and bracelets of fine white beads; there was also by it a little bow, about three quarters long, and some other odd knacks. We brought sundry of the prettiest things away with us, and covered the corpse up again. After this, we digged in sundry like places, but found no more corn, nor any thing else but graves.

The lack of regard for Native burials was an extension of the belief that Native people were fundamentally different from White people, and less than fully human, whether because of their lack of Christianity or, by the mid-nineteenth century, because of their alleged biological inferiority. As the conquest of Native people spread across the continent, their graves became the targets of relic hunters and scientists. By the 1870s, teams from the Smithsonian trailed the US Cavalry on the Great Plains, decapitating Indian corpses on battlefields and massacre sites and shipping the heads back to Washington, where scientists would use them as "evidence" to support racist theories claiming Native people were a less evolved, degenerate version of humanity. Burial grounds were looted to feed the growing market in antiquities, or, in the twentieth century, opened to view and promoted as tourist attractions.

In New Hampshire, Native American burials were encountered throughout the eighteenth and nineteenth centuries, sometimes occasioning brief mention in local histories. With the growth of local historical societies and museums in the late-nineteenth century, these remains, which had previously been discarded with little or no record, were now placed in collections and put on public display. In 1873, the skeletons of a man and a woman, wrapped in bark with their knees tucked up to their chest, were uncovered in Laconia during the excavation of a cellar. They were removed and sold for $12.00 to the Philomathic Club (later the New Hampshire Antiquarian Society) in Hopkinton. Here they remained for decades, part of the collection of curiosities and antiquities, until a new curator decided to remove them from the collection in the 1950s.

The remains of these two people were then thrown in the town dump.

Sometimes the prevailing attitude about Indians and their remains led to behavior that would be called criminally insane had it taken place in a White cemetery. In June 1959, during construction at a house site in Wayland, Massachusetts, a bulldozer plowed up the remains of a 3,500-year-old burial ground, including hundreds of stone tools, soapstone pots, artifacts of copper from the

Great Lakes, and partially cremated human bone. Word spread quickly, and dozens of people, including avocational archaeologists from the Massachusetts Archaeological Society and entire families with pickaxes, shovels, and picnic baskets, descended on the site, completely looting it in a festive free-for-all over the course of a few days.

By the 1960s, the civil rights movement had empowered a new generation of Native activists for whom the protection of sacred sites and burial grounds was a central issue. As a result, in 1990 Congress passed the Native American Graves Protection and Repatriation Act (NAGPRA), which required that museums provide a list of all human remains, grave goods, and sacred objects to the tribes whose territories they had come from. This allowed the tribes to request their return, or repatriation, beginning a nationwide review of museum collections and the return of thousands of items to Native tribes. This required archaeologists to work directly with Native people, to share information, and to build relationships where none had existed. In doing so, we also learned, to our surprise, that Native people often had information about their own history that complimented and sometimes challenged the stories told by archaeological science, and that's what had led me to Nanepashemet's office.

For the Abenaki people of New Hampshire and Vermont, NAGPRA seemed to exclude them, as tribes were defined in the legislation as only those groups who had received recognition from the federal government. While recognition often came with the imposition of federal control over tribes, it also granted a degree of autonomy, including in matters of historic preservation, with the Tribal Historic Preservation Office having equivalent powers to a State Historic Preservation office in managing the archaeological resources of the tribe.

The Abenaki, lacking any formal reservation and effectively hidden from sight by the early nineteenth century, had never received recognition. In 1982, the Missisquoi Abenaki community around Swanton, Vermont, became the first and only Western Abenaki group to apply for federal recognition. Twenty-five years after their initial submission, the application was denied, with the Department of the Interior ruling that they had not met the requirements of showing documentary evidence of tribal membership and unbroken descent from a historic Indian tribe. For people who were historically organized into highly autonomous local communities and family groups, whose survival depended on hiding their Indian identity, these requirements were almost tailor-made to deny them recognition and, with it, their right to speak for themselves under NAGPRA.

Despite this, Abenaki activists have worked hard for the return of Abenaki remains from museums, historical societies, and colleges and universities. In 1996, under the leadership of Repatriation Coordinator Donna Moody, the Abenaki Nation of Missisquoi became the first non-recognized Native group to receive ancestral remains under NAGPRA when the Hood Museum at Dartmouth College returned the remains of an Abenaki child unearthed on the shore of Lake Winnipesaukee. The lack of federal recognition requires that all Abenaki remains be identified in official NAGPRA documents as "Culturally Unaffiliated" (with Western Abenaki added in parenthesis), and each repatriation request must be reviewed and approved by recognized tribes elsewhere in New England, typically the Wampanoag in southeastern Massachusetts and the federally recognized tribes in Maine. While these peoples are closely related to the Western Abenaki and have always supported their cousins' requests, it can extend the process of repatriating even a single set of remains by a year or more.

Fortunately, human remains are rarely encountered on archaeological sites in New Hampshire, and these days when they are, every effort is made to preserve them in place, or to turn them over to the Abenaki for reburial. I have worked on sites with skeletons eroding from riverbanks, in crawl spaces under lakeside vacation cabins, and in piles of soil deposited in gravel pits by dump trucks. In each case, this work had been overseen by the state archaeologist in consultation with Abenaki people and has resulted in the return of the remains to the Abenaki for reburial. I have also had the honor of participating in a number of these reburials, reversing the normal work of an archaeologist by putting people's remains back into the earth.

In the absence of federal recognition, Vermont extended state recognition to the Abenaki in 1976, which was repealed the following year when a new, Republican governor took office. The possibility of state recognition was restored in 2011, and, to date, four Abenaki groups have applied for and received this status, which does bring limited privileges, including the right to sell traditional crafts with the designation "Indian Made." In New Hampshire, with its more conservative political culture, no effort to recognize the Abenaki has ever been seriously considered. In 2010, however, the legislature did create the New Hampshire Native American Affairs Commission to "recognize the historic and cultural contributions of Native Americans to New Hampshire, to promote and strengthen their own heritage, and to further their needs through state policy and programs." The commission included five members appointed by various state agencies and ten Native American members chosen by the Native community.

I was chosen by the New Hampshire Division of Historic Resources as one of the charter members of the commission, and I served for the next six years. In its creation of the commission, the legislature was very careful to avoid language that would recognize the Abenaki as the original inhabitants of the state, fearing this might support any later claim for federal recognition. The name Abenaki does not appear anywhere in the legislation creating the commission, showing that the centuries-long effort to ensure their invisibility is alive and well.

In a world controlled by powerful, centralized institutions, the lack of an official, centralized leadership structure has made it harder for the Abenaki to achieve their goals and more difficult for their non-Native allies to support them. The modern Abenaki population is fractious, divided into small groups that spend too much time and energy arguing with each other, making it easy for outsiders to dismiss them, or to pick and choose the most pliable person or group to work with, pursuing the age-old strategy of controlling people by keeping them divided. But this lack of centralized control may also reflect the endurance of ancient tradition, as the Abenaki have always lived in small, autonomous groups, bound together more by ties of kinship and common culture than by allegiance to a single ruler or government.

CHAPTER 9

Conclusion

Figure 9.1. Nulhegan Abenaki basket maker Sherry Gould teaching young people to make baskets. (Photograph by Bill Gould. Courtesy of Sherry Gould.)

In 2008, my friend and colleague Gail Golec, who has spent years documenting archaeological sites around Bellows Falls, located on the Connecticut River between New Hampshire and Vermont, shared an interesting story. A local history, published in 1907, recounted that many of the older residents in town remembered that up until the mid-1850s Abenaki people still came back occasionally

125

from Quebec to spend the summer and early fall around Bellows Falls and the surrounding area. Small groups of Abenaki would camp on either side of the river above the falls on the outskirts of town, fish, and sell baskets to local residents. This account claimed the last Native family came to the area in 1856, when an old man, his wife, and their two sons arrived in town. When asked why they had come, the old man said he wanted to die and be left with his ancestors, and his family set up camp along Governors' Brook in North Walpole and stayed all summer and into the fall. He died late in the fall and was buried in an unmarked grave in the Catholic cemetery in Bellows Falls, only a short distance from where those enigmatic faces carved on a rock ledge watch the water cascade southwards on its way through Ndakinna.

Were these really the last Abenaki people to come to Bellows Falls? While many town histories deny the existence of the Abenaki, the ones that don't often bring their history to an end with romantic stories of the "Last Indian," thereby denying their existence in the present. This fiction had been put to rest by a renaissance in the last fifty years in which Abenaki activists, elders, scholars, linguists, and artists have revitalized their culture and obliged the rest of the world to acknowledge their long presence in this region and the remarkable story of their survival. The history, archaeology, and experiences of Native people reveal ancient continuities and traditions embedded in a web of kinship and culture that spans thousands of miles, a deep presence that has somehow survived the awful trials of history and the modern age. This is the story that is worth telling, and retelling, even as it continues to unfold.

Bibliography and Sources

Chapter 1. Introduction

Brooks, Lisa, Donna Moody, and John Moody. 2009. "Native Space." In *Where the Great River Rises*. Rebecca Brown, ed., pp. 133–137. Hanover, NH: University of New England Press.

Bunker, Victoria. 2007. "Time and Place: The Archaeology of the Eddy Site." *The New Hampshire Archeologist 46–47*.

Griffin, Simon. 1904. *Upper Ashuelot: A History of the Town of Keene*. Keene, NH: Sentinel Printing Company.

Haviland, William and Marjory Power. 1994. *The Original Vermonters: Native Inhabitants, Past and Present*. Hanover, NH: University Press of New England.

Haviland, William and Marjory Power. 1995. "Visions in Stone: A New Look at the Bellows Falls Petroglyphs." *Northeast Anthropology* 50:91–108.

On the Abenaki meaning of the name Monadnock: Jesse Bruchac, personal communication, February 10, 2021.

Chapter 2. Who Are the Native People?

Beck, Jane. 1972. "The Giant Beaver: A Prehistoric Memory?" *Ethnohistory* 19(2):109–122.

Brooks, Lisa. 2018. *Our Beloved Kin: A New History of King Philip's War*. New Haven, CT: Yale University Press.

Calloway, Colin. 1990. *The Western Abenakis of Vermont, 1600–1800*. Norman, OK: University of Oklahoma Press.

Day, Gordon. 1965. "The Identity of the Sokokis." *Ethnohistory 12(3):237–249*.

Day, Gordon. 1978. "Western Abenaki." In *Handbook of North American Indians, Vol. 15: Northeast.* B. Trigger, ed. Washington, DC: Smithsonian Institution.

Greenberg, J. H., C. G. Turner, and S. L. Zegura. 1986. "The Settlement of the Americas: A Comparison of the Linguistic, Dental, and Genetic Evidence." *Current Anthropology* 27(5):477–497.

Lacy, David and Donna Roberts Moody. 2006. "Green Mountain Stewardship: One Landscape, Multiple Histories." In *Cross-Cultural Collaboration: Native Peoples and Archaeology in the Northeastern United States.* J. Kerber, ed. Lincoln, NE: University of Nebraska Press.

Moody, John. 2011. "Balance: An Overview of Abenaki and Indigenous Peoples, Burial/Site Protection, Repatriation, and Customs of Respect, Looting, and Site Destruction in the Abenaki Homeland, and Relations between Archeology, Ethnohistory, and Traditional Knowledge." *Journal of Vermont Archaeology* 12:46–84.

Stewart-Smith, David. 1994. "The Penacook: Lands and Relations, an Ethnography." *The New Hampshire Archeologist* 33/34:66–80.

Strong, W. D. 1934. "North American Indian Traditions Suggesting a Knowledge of the Mammoth." *American Anthropologist* 36(1):81–88.

Chapter 3. Opening the Puzzle

Abrams, Mark and Gregory Nowacki. 2020. "Native American Imprint in Palaeoecology." *Nature Sustainability* 3:896–897.

Boisvert, Richard. 1992. "The Mount Jasper Lithic Source, Berlin, New Hampshire: National Register of Historic Places Nomination and Commentary." *Archaeology of Eastern North America* 20:151–166.

Boudreau, Jeff. 2008. *A New England Typology of Native American Projectile Points.* Ashland, MA: Freedom Digital.

Braun, David. 1983. "Pots as Tools." In *Archaeological Hammers and Theories.* J. Moore and A. Keene, eds., pp. 107–134. New York: Academic Press.

Bunker, Victoria. 2002. "Analysis and Interpretation of Early Ceramics from Sewalls and Amoskeag Falls, Merrimack River Valley, New Hampshire." In

A Lasting Impression: Coastal, Lithic, and Ceramic Research in New England Archaeology. J. Kerber, ed. Westport, CT: Praeger Publishers.

Bunker, Victoria. 2007. "Time and Place: The Archaeology of the Eddy Site." *The New Hampshire Archeologist* 46–47.

Dincauze, Dena. 1976. *The Neville Site: 8,000 Years at Amoskeag, Manchester, New Hampshire.* Peabody Museum Monographs No.4. Cambridge, MA: Harvard University.

Duggan, Colleen. 1997. "Dugout Canoes of New Hampshire." *The New Hampshire Archeologist* 37.

Ewing, Robert and Charles Bolian. 1991. "Argillite Workshops in Tamworth, New Hampshire." *The New Hampshire Archeologist* 32:87–95.

Goodby, Robert. 1994. *Style, Meaning, and History: A Contextual Study of 17th Century Native American Ceramics from Southeastern New England* (unpublished PhD diss., Department of Anthropology, Brown University).

Goodby, Robert. 2001. "Defining the Dynamic Late Archaic Period at the Davison Brook Site, 27GR201." *The New Hampshire Archeologist* 41:1–87.

Goodby, Robert. 2002. "Reconsidering the Shantok Tradition." In *A Lasting Impression: Coastal, Lithic and Ceramic Research in New England Archaeology.* J. Kerber, ed. Westport, CT: Bergin & Garvey.

Goodby, Robert. 2005. *Phase IB Intensive Archaeological Investigation and Phase II Determination of Eligibility Study, Holderness Village Sidewalk Project, Holderness, New Hampshire (05022).* Stoddard, NH: Monadnock Archaeological Consulting, LLC.

Goodby, Robert. 2011. "Soft Stone in Dalton." In *Beyond the Notches: Stories of Place in New Hampshire's North Country.* Littleton, NH: Bondcliff Books.

Goodby, Robert. 2013. "Jack's Reef Points in Northern New England: Exotic Lithics and Long-Distance Interaction in the Post-Hopewell Northeast." *Archaeology of Eastern North America* 41:59–67.

Heckenberger, M. J., J. B. Petersen, L. A. Basa, E. R. Cowie, A. E. Spiess, and R. E. Stuckenrath. 1990. "Early Woodland Period Mortuary Ceremonialism in the Far Northeast: A View from the Boucher Cemetery." *Archaeology of Eastern North America* 18:109–144.

Howe, Dennis. 2000. "A View of Middle Archaic Life from Lithic Workshops." *The New Hampshire Archeologist* 40:1–42.

Ives, Timothy and Alan Leveille. 2005. "Busy in the Shadow of the Ossipee Mountains: Archaic Hornfels Workshops and a Paleoindian Site in Tamworth, NH." *The New Hampshire Archeologist* 45:1–29.

Kenyon, Victoria. 1983. *River Valleys and Human Interaction: A Critical Evaluation of Middle Woodland Ceramics in the Merrimack River Valley.* (unpublished PhD diss., Boston University).

Kenyon, Victoria and Patricia McDowell. 1983. "Environmental Setting of Merrimack River Valley Prehistoric Sites." *Man in the Northeast* 25:7–23.

King, Adam and James Hatch. 1997. "The Chemical Composition of Jasper Artefacts from New England and the Middle Atlantic: Implications for the Prehistoric Exchange of Pennsylvania Jasper." *Journal of Archaeological Science* 24:793–812.

Luedtke, Barbara. 1987. "The Pennsylvania Connection: Jasper at Massachusetts Sites." *Bulletin of the Massachusetts Archeological Society* 48(2):37–47.

Loring, Stephen. 2017. "To the Uttermost Ends of the Earth...Ramah Chert in Time and Space." In *Ramah Chert: a Lithic Odyssey.* Jenneth Curtis and Pierre Desrosiers, eds., pp. 169–219. Westmount, Quebec: Avataq Cultural Institute.

Patterson, William and Kenneth Sassaman. 1988. "Indian Fires in the Prehistory of New England." In *Holocene Human Ecology in Northeastern North America*, George Nicholas, ed., pp. 107–135. Boston, MA: Springer.

Petersen, James and Nathan D. Hamilton. 1984. "Early Woodland Ceramic and Perishable Fiber Industries from the Northeast: A Summary and Interpretation." *Annals of the Carnegie Museum* 53(14):413–445.

Petersen, James, John Crock, Ellen Cowie, Richard Boisvert, Joshua Toney, and Geoff Mandel. 2004. "St. Lawrence Iroquoians in Northern New England: Pendergast was 'Right' and More." In *A Passion for the Past: Papers in Honour of James F. Pendergast.* James V. Wright and Jean-Luc Pilon, eds. Archaeological Survey of Canada Mercury Series Paper 164. Gatineau, Quebec: Canadian Museum of Civilization, pp. 107–153.

Petersen, James and Joshua Toney. 2000. "Three Native American Ceramic Vessels from Western Vermont: The Colchester and Bolton Jars Revisited." *Journal of Vermont Archaeology* 3:2–16.

Pollock, Stephen, Nathan Hamilton, and Richard Boisvert. 2007. "Archaeological Geology of Two Flow-Banded Spherulitic Rhyolites in New England, USA: Their History, Exploitation and Criteria for Recognition." *Journal of Archaeological Science* 35(3):688-703.

Pollock, Stephen, Nathan Hamilton, and Robson Bonnichsen. 1999. "Chert from the Munsungen Lake Formation (Maine) in Paleoamerican Archaeological Sites in Northeastern North America: Recognition of its Occurrence and Distribution." *Journal of Archaeological Science* 26:269–293.

Ritchie, William. 1971. *A Typology and Nomenclature for New York State Projectile Points*. New York State Museum and Science Service Bulletin, 384.

Robinson, Brian. 1992. "Early and Middle Archaic Period Occupation in the Gulf of Maine Region: Mortuary and Technological Patterning." In *Early Holocene Occupation in Northern New England*. Occasional Publications in Maine Archaeology 9:63–116.

Sargent, Howard and Francois Ledoux. 1973. "Two Fluted Points from New England." *Man in the Northeast* 5:67–68.

Snow, Dean. 1980. *The Archaeology of New England*. New York: Academic Press.

Walker, Robert, Kim Hill, Mark Flinn, and Ryan Ellsworth. 2011. "Evolutionary History of Hunter-Gatherer Marriage Practices." PLoS ONE 6(4):e19066. doi:10.1371/journal.pone.0019066.

Williams, Roger. 1973. *A Key Into the Language of America*. Detroit, MI: Wayne State University Press.

Chapter 4. A Dam in the River

Brooks, Lisa, Donna Moody, and John Moody. "Native Space." In *Where the Great River Rises*. Rebecca Brown, ed., pp. 133–137. Hanover, NH: University of New England Press.

Carlson, Catherine. 1988. "Where's the Salmon? A Reevaluation of the Role of Anadromous Fisheries to Aboriginal New England." In *Human Holocene*

Ecology in Northeastern North America. George P. Nicholas, ed., pp. 47–80. New York: Plenum Press.

Cook, Thomas. 1976. "Broadpoint: Culture, Phase, Horizon, Tradition, or Knife?" *Journal of Anthropological Research* 32:337–357.

Curran, Mary Lou. 1984. "The Whipple Site and Paleo-Indian Tool Assemblage Variation: A Comparison of Intrasite Structuring." *Archaeology of Eastern North America* 12:5–40.

Curran, Mary Lou. 1994. "New Hampshire Paleo-Indian Research and the Whipple Site." *The New Hampshire Archaeologist* 33/34:29–52.

Custer, John. 1991. "Notes on Broadspear Functions." *Archaeology of Eastern North America* 19:51–73.

Goodby, Robert. 2006. "11,000 Years on the Ashuelot." In *Where the Mountain Stands Alone: Stories of Place in the Monadnock Region*. Howard Mansfield, ed., pp. 33–43. Hanover, NH: University Press of New England.

Goodby, Robert, Sarah Tremblay, and Edward Bouras. 2015. "The Swanzey Fish Dam: A Large, Pre-Contact Native American Stone Structure in South-western New Hampshire." *Northeast Anthropology* 81-82:1–22.

Gookin, Daniel. 1792. "Historical Collections of the Indians in New England." *Collections of the Massachusetts Historical Society* 1:141–227.

Griffin, Simon. 1904. *A History of the Town of Keene*. Sentinel Printing Company, Keene, NH. (Griffin's description of the dam includes the quotation from the 1888 article by George Wheelock that appeared in the *New England Observer*.)

Ogden, Quinn-Monique. 2004. *The Swanzey Fish Dam in Comparison to Native Dams across Eastern North America* (unpublished senior thesis, Department of Anthropology, Franklin Pierce College, Rindge, NH).

Price, Chester. 1967. "Historic Indian Trails of New Hampshire." *The New Hampshire Archeologist* 14:1–12.

Chapter 5. A Knoll in the Forest

Lacy, David. 1997. "Rocks, Space and the Organization of Production at a Prehistoric Quartzite Quarry." *Journal of Vermont Archaeology* 2:37–42.

Milne, Claudia and Suzanne Cherau. 1999. *Historical and Archeological Reconnaissance Survey: Edward McDowell Lake, Volumes I and II.* Pawtucket, RI: The Public Archaeology Laboratory, Inc.

Rainville, Celine, Tonya Largy, and Robert Goodby. 2012. "The Raft Bridge Site (27HB299): A Multi-Component Site in Peterborough, New Hampshire." *The New Hampshire Archeologist* 52:1–17.

Chapter 6. The Snakes of Wantastiquet

Brattleboro Reformer. 1886. "Untitled." 16 September. Retrieved from http://brattleborohistory.com/plants-animals/rattlesnakes-on-wantastiquet.html, accessed February 18, 2013.

Brooks, Lisa, Donna Moody, and John Moody. 2009. "Native Space." In *Where the Great River Rises.* Rebecca Brown, ed., pp. 133–137. Hanover, NH: University of New England Press.

Childs, Frederick. 1883. "Sees Snakes." *Brattleboro Reformer.* August 24. Retrieved from http://brattleborohistory.com/plants-animals/rattle-snakes-on-wantastiquet.html, accessed February 18, 2013.

Clifford, Brendan. 2019. "Don't Be Rattled! Examining New Hampshire's Isolated and Fragile Timber Rattlesnake Population." *New Hampshire Wildlife Journal* May/June pp. 6–11.

Goodby, Robert, Tonya Largy, Van Wallach, and Alyssa Bergquist. 2020. "Native American Use of Venomous Snakes at the Wantastiquet Mountain Site (27CH89), Hinsdale, New Hampshire." *Archaeology of Eastern North America* 48:23–35.

Hamell, George and William Fox. 2005. "Rattlesnake Tales." *Ontario Archaeology* 79/80:127–149.

Heckenberger, M. J., J. B. Petersen, L. A. Basa, E. R. Cowie, A. E. Spiess, and R. E. Stuckenrath. 1990. "Early Woodland Period Mortuary

Ceremonialism in the Far Northeast: A View from the Boucher Cemetery." *Archaeology of Eastern North America* 18:109–144.

Laurent, Joseph. 1884. *New Familiar Abenakis and English Dialogues*. Quebec: Leger Brousseau.

Minton, Sherman and Madge Minton. 1980. *Venomous Reptiles (Revised Edition)*. New York: Charles Scribner and Sons.

Palmer, Thomas. 1992. *Landscape with Reptile*. New York: Ticknor and Fields.

Rubio, Manny. 1998. *Rattlesnake: Portrait of a Predator*. Smithsonian Institution Press, Washington, DC.

Chapter 7. Where it All Began

Boisvert, Richard. 1999. "Paleoindian Occupation of the White Mountains, New Hampshire." *Geographie physique et Quaternaire* 53(1):159–174.

Boisvert, Richard. 2004. "Clovis-era Archaeology in Northern New Hampshire: The Israel River Complex." In *New Perspectives on the First Americans*, pp. 49–54. College Station, TX: Texas A & M University Press.

Chilton, Elizabeth. 1994. "In Search of Paleo-Women: Gender Implications of Remains from Paleoindian Sites in the Northeast." *Bulletin of the Massachusetts Archaeological Society* 55(1):8–14.

Goodby, Robert. 2009. *Phase IA Archaeological Sensitivity Assessment and Phase IB Intensive Archaeological Investigation, Proposed Keene Middle School Site, Maple Avenue, Keene, New Hampshire*. Stoddard, NH: Monadnock Archaeological Consulting, LLC.

Goodby, Robert. 2010. *Phase II Determination of Eligibility Study, Site 27CH187, Proposed Keene Middle School Site, Maple Avenue, Keene, New Hampshire*. Stoddard, NH: Monadnock Archaeological Consulting, LLC.

Goodby, Robert, Paul Bock, Edward Bouras, Christopher Dorion, A. Garrett Evans, Tonya Largy, Steven Pollock, and Heather Rockwell. 2011. *Phase III Data Recovery at the Tenant Swamp Site (27CH187), Keene Middle School Site, Maple Avenue, Keene, New Hampshire*. Stoddard, NH: Monadnock Archaeological Consulting, LLC.

Goodby, Robert, Paul Bock, Edward Bouras, Christopher Dorion, A. Garrett Evans, Tonya Largy, Stephen Pollock, Heather Rockwell, and Arthur Spiess. 2014. "The Tenant Swamp Site and Paleoindian Domestic Space in Keene, New Hampshire." *Archaeology of Eastern North America* 42:129–164.

Gramly, Richard. 1982. "The Vail Site: A Paleo-Indian Encampment in Maine." *Bulletin of the Buffalo Society of Natural Sciences*, Vol. 30.

Hodge, Frederick. 1907. *Handbook of American Indians North of Mexico*. Washington, DC: Government Printing Office.

McKeon, J. B. 1989. "Late-Glacial Dunes, Ventifacts, and Wind Direction in West-Central Maine." *Studies in Maine Geology* 6:89–101.

Pollock, Stephen, Nathan Hamilton, and Richard Boisvert. 2007. "Archaeological Geology of Two Flow-Banded Spherulitic Rhyolites in New England, USA: Their History, Exploitation and Criteria for Recognition." *Journal of Archaeological Science*, 35(3):688–703.

Pollock, Stephen, Nathan Hamilton, and Robson Bonnichsen. 1999. "Chert from the Munsungen Lake Formation (Maine) in Paleoamerican Archaeological Sites in Northeastern North America: Recognition of its Occurrence and Distribution." *Journal of Archaeological Science* 26:269–293.

Walker, Robert, Kim Hill, Mark Flinn, and Ryan Ellsworth. 2011. "Evolutionary History of Hunter-Gatherer Marriage Practices." PLoS ONE 6(4):e19066. doi:10.1371/journal.pone.0019066.

Chapter 8. Survival, Resistance, Renaissance

Archer, John. 1983. *The New Hampshire Antiquarian Society: Its Story.* Hopkinton, NH: New Hampshire Antiquarian Society.

Ball, Margaret. 2013. *Grim Commerce: Scalps, Bounties, and the Transformation of Trophy-Taking in the Early American Northeast, 1450–1770.* (unpublished PhD diss., Department of History, University of Colorado).

Bragdon, Kathleen. 1996. *Native People of Southern New England 1500–1650.* Norman, OK: University of Oklahoma Press.

Brooks, Lisa. 2018. *Our Beloved Kin: A New History of King Philip's War.* New Haven, CT: Yale University Press.

Bruchac, Marge. 2006. "Sokoki Homeland from Monadnock: K'namitobena Sokwaki." In *Where the Mountain Stands Alone*. Howard Mansfield, ed. Hanover: University Press of New England.

Bureau of Indian Affairs. 2007. *Summary Under the Criteria and Evidence for Final Determination Against Federal Acknowledgement of the St. Francis/ Sokoki Band of Abenakis of Vermont*. Washington, DC: Bureau of Indian Affairs.

Byers, Douglas. 1960. "The Rape of Wayland." *American Antiquity* 25(3):420.

Calloway, Colin, ed. 1997. *After King Philip's War: Presence and Persistence in Indian New England*. Hanover, NH: University Press of New England.

Chabot, Nancy Jo. Personal communication, January 2021.

Gallagher, Nancy. 1999. *Breeding Better Vermonters: The Eugenics Project in the Green Mountain State*. Hanover, NH: University of New England Press.

Goodby, Robert. 2006. "Working with the Abenaki in New Hampshire." In *Cross-Cultural Collaboration: Native Peoples and Archaeology in the Northeastern United States*. J. Kerber, ed. Lincoln, NE: University of Nebraska Press.

Heath, Dwight, ed. 1986. *Mourt's Relation: A Journal of the Pilgrims at Plymouth*. Bedford, MA: Applewood Books.

Kerr, Ronald. 1999. *Indian New England 1524–1674: A Compendium of Eyewitness Accounts of Native American Life*. Pepperell, MA: Branch Line Press.

Ketchum, Silas. *Exposition of the Philomathic Club: A Catalogue of the Curious and Antique Articles in Its Possession*. Bristol, NH: George Crowell Ketchum, Printer.

Lebanon Historical Society. 2006. "On Gypsies in Lebanon, NH." http://www.lebanonnhhistory.org/ exhibits/historic-features/east-leb.html, accessed November 2006.

Marr, John and John Cathey. 2010. "New Hypothesis for Cause of Epidemic among Native Americans, New England, 1616–1619." *Emerging Infectious Diseases* 16:2.

Moody, John. 2011. "Balance: An Overview of Abenaki and Indigenous Peoples, Burial/Site Protection, Repatriation, and Customs of Respect, Looting, and Site Destruction in the Abenaki Homeland, and Relations between Archeology, Ethnohistory, and Traditional Knowledge." *Journal of Vermont Archaeology* 12:46–84.

Murphy, Lynn, guest curator. 2017. "Persistence of Identity." Exhibit at the Mt. Kearsarge Indian Museum, Warner, NH.

Parker, Trudy Ann. 1994. *Aunt Sarah: Woman of the Dawnland*. Lancaster, NH: Dawnland Publications.

Salisbury, Neal. *Manitou and Providence: Indians, Europeans, and the Making of New England 1500–1643*. New York: Oxford University Press.

Spiess, Arthur, and Spiess, B. 1987. "New England Pandemic of 1616–1622: Cause and Archeological Implication." *Man in the Northeast* 34:71–83.

Thomas, David Hurst. 2001. *Skull Wars: Kennewick Man, Archaeology, and the Battle for Native American Identity*. New York: Basic Books.

Thomas, Peter. 1991. *In the Maelstrom of Change: The Indian Trade and Cultural Process in the Middle Connecticut River Valley, 1635–1665*. London: Garland Science Publishers.

Turnbaugh, Sarah, and William Turnbaugh. 2015. *Indian Basketry of the Northeastern Woodlands*. Atglen, PA: Schiffer Publishing, Ltd.

Chapter 9. Conclusion

Hayes, L. S. 1907. *History of the Town of Rockingham, Vermont, Including the Villages of: Bellows Falls, Saxtons River, Rockingham, Cambridgeport and Bartonsville 1753–1907*. Lyman, MA: Frank S. Whitten.

About the Author

(Photograph by James Van Campen.)

Robert Goodby is Professor of Anthropology at Franklin Pierce University. He earned his PhD in anthropology from Brown University and has over thirty years of experience excavating Native American archaeological sites in New England. He is a past president of the New Hampshire Archeological Society, a former Trustee of the Mt. Kearsarge Indian Museum, and served on the New Hampshire Commission on Native American Affairs. He has directed over three hundred archaeological studies authorized by the National Historic Preservation Act and his work has appeared in anthropological journals and in anthologies published by the Smithsonian Institution Press and University Press of New England. He has presented more than one hundred talks on his archaeological research for the New Hampshire Humanities "Humanities to Go" program, and every fall speaks to students at the Keene Middle School about the Paleoindian Tenant Swamp Site.